Peter Stimpson

Cambridge International AS and A Level
Business
Workbook

CAMBRIDGE
UNIVERSITY PRESS

University Printing House, Cambridge CB2 8BS, United Kingdom

One Liberty Plaza, 20th Floor, New York, NY 10006, USA

477 Williamstown Road, Port Melbourne, VIC 3207, Australia

314–321, 3rd Floor, Plot 3, Splendor Forum, Jasola District Centre, New Delhi – 110025, India

79 Anson Road, 06 -04/06, Singapore 079906

Cambridge University Press is part of the University of Cambridge.

It furthers the University's mission by disseminating knowledge in the pursuit of education, learning and research at the highest international levels of excellence.

Information on this title: cambridge.org/9781108401579

© Cambridge University Press 2018

This publication is in copyright. Subject to statutory exception and to the provisions of relevant collective licensing agreements, no reproduction of any part may take place without the written permission of Cambridge University Press.

First published 2018

20 19 18 17 16 15 14 13 12 11 10 9 8 7 6 5 4

Printed in Great Britain by CPI Group (UK) Ltd, Croydon CR0 4YY

A catalogue record for this publication is available from the British Library

ISBN 978-1-108-40157-9 Paperback

Additional resources for this publication at cambridge.org/9781108401579

Cambridge University Press has no responsibility for the persistence or accuracy of URLs for external or third-party internet websites referred to in this publication, and does not guarantee that any content on such websites is, or will remain, accurate or appropriate. Information regarding prices, travel timetables, and other factual information given in this work is correct at the time of first printing but Cambridge University Press does not guarantee the accuracy of such information thereafter.

All examination-style questions, sample mark schemes, solutions and/or comments that appear in this book were written by the author. In examination, the way marks would be awarded to answers like these may be different.

....

NOTICE TO TEACHERS IN THE UK
It is illegal to reproduce any part of this work in material form (including photocopying and electronic storage) except under the following circumstances:
(i) where you are abiding by a licence granted to your school or institution by the Copyright Licensing Agency;
(ii) where no such licence exists, or where you wish to exceed the terms of a licence, and you have gained the written permission of Cambridge University Press;
(iii) where you are allowed to reproduce without permission under the provisions of Chapter 3 of the Copyright, Designs and Patents Act 1988, which covers, for example, the reproduction of short passages within certain types of educational anthology and reproduction for the purposes of setting examination questions.

Contents

Introduction	v
How to use this book	vi

Unit 1 Business and its environment — 1

1	Enterprise	2
2	Business structure	6
3	Size of business	10
4	Business objectives	14
5	Stakeholders in a business	18
6	Business structure (A Level)	22
7	Size of business (A Level)	26
8	External influences on business activity (A Level only)	30
9	External economic influences on business behaviour (A Level only)	34

Unit 2 People in organisations — 40

10	Management and leadership	41
11	Motivation	45
12	Human resource management	50
13	Further human resource management (A Level only)	54
14	Organisational structure (A Level only)	59
15	Business communication (A Level only)	64

Unit 3 Marketing — 69

16	What is marketing?	70
17	Market research	75
18	The marketing mix – product and price	80
19	The marketing mix – promotion and place	85
20	Marketing planning (A Level only)	89
21	Globalisation and international marketing (A Level only)	94

Cambridge AS and A Level Business

Unit 4 Operations and project management — 99

22 The nature of operations — 100

23 Operations planning (AS and A Level) — 105

24 Inventory management — 110

25 Capacity utilisation (A Level only) — 114

26 Lean production and quality management (A Level only) — 118

27 Project management (A Level only) — 122

Unit 5 Finance and accounting — 128

28 Business finance — 129

29 Costs — 134

30 Accounting fundamentals — 139

31 Forecasting and managing cash flows — 145

32 Costs (A Level only) — 150

33 Budgets (A Level only) — 155

34 Contents of published accounts (A Level only) — 160

35 Analysis of published accounts (A Level only) — 165

36 Investment appraisal (A Level only) — 170

Unit 6 Strategic management — 176

37 What is strategic management? (A Level only) — 177

38 Strategic analysis (A Level only) — 182

39 Strategic choice (A Level only) — 188

40 Strategic implementation (A Level only) — 193

Introduction

This workbook is designed to help you develop your knowledge of Business as you study for the Cambridge International AS and A Level qualifications. Working through it will help you feel much more confident about what you need to know to be a successful student of Business.

A unique feature of the workbook is that it includes a range of exercises in every chapter that will enable you to build up your core skills. It is important that you gain as much practice as possible in developing these skills which are:

- Knowledge and understanding
- Application of knowledge and understanding
- Analysis
- Evaluation

This workbook is a key member of the Cambridge University Press 'family' of supportive materials for students of Business following the Cambridge International AS and A level qualifications. You will gain most benefit from the workbook by combining your study of Business with the two other books that Cambridge University Press publishes to support AS and A level students:

Endorsed textbook: Cambridge International AS and A level Business Coursebook (Stimpson and Farquharson; 2014; ISBN 978-1107677364)

Endorsed revision guide: Cambridge International AS and A level Business Revision Guide (Stimpson and Joyce; 2017; ISBN 978-1316611708).

Answers to the all exam-style questions are provided online at cambridge.org/9781108401579 to allow both students and their teachers to have access to the ways in which each question should be responded to. Most of these are in outline form. They are not designed to be complete answers, but to provide a framework within which the key points can be explained by students as they write out their full responses. Some answers to exercises and exam-style questions are given in a complete form to demonstrate the length and content of good exam-style responses. These are also annotated with the abbreviations K; Ap; An and E to indicate the key assessment skills that the answers contain.

Students are encouraged to complete their own answers before referring to these outlines or these complete/annotated answers. The more practice gained at responding to exam-style questions the better your answers will become!

How to use this book

This book is designed as a practical workbook to help you put into practice the knowledge and skills you learn as you progress through your Cambridge International AS and A Level Business course.

Throughout this book you will notice recurring features that are designed to help your learning. Here is a brief overview of what you'll find.

Learning outcomes – Each chapter begins by outlining the key learning aims for each topic. These will help you to navigate through the content in the book (these also map to the content in the Coursebook).

1 Enterprise

Learning outcomes

The exercises in this chapter will help you to practice what you have learnt about:

- What is meant by business activity
- Analysing opportunity cost and the economic problem
- How businesses can create value
- Applying the characteristics of successful entrepreneurs
- Analysing why new businesses can fail
- The importance of enterprise and entrepreneurs to a country's economy
- The objectives (triple bottom line) and roles of social enterprises.

Key terms – A reminder of the key vocabulary for each chapter topic as you work through the exercises and exam-style questions.

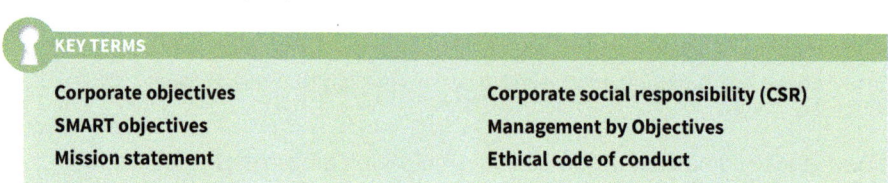

KEY TERMS

Corporate objectives	Corporate social responsibility (CSR)
SMART objectives	Management by Objectives
Mission statement	Ethical code of conduct

Tip – Tips are in place to provide you with additional practical guidance and advice in approaching exercises and exam-style questions.

TIP

For Q11, calculate total market sales this year by adding 10% of last year's total sales to last year's total sales; then use the market share formula using RCE's forecast sales for this year.

How to use this book

Worked example – Worked examples provide you with sample answers, to help you understand how to answer questions using key skills.

> **WORKED EXAMPLE**
>
> SCT operates old trains. This might increase profits for shareholders in the short term as the business does not use profits to buy new trains **[Ap]** – benefiting shareholders as business profits is a major objective for this group. **[K]** However, old trains are polluting **[Ap]** and this is damaging the health of the train workers – who have the objective of a safe and clean working environment. **[K]**

Key skills exercises – Scaffolded exercises support you as you progress through your course. They have been clearly linked to the key skills you need as a student of business, to allow you to put into practice what you have learnt on your course so far.

> ## Key skills exercises
>
> ### Knowledge and understanding
>
> **To answer the questions in this chapter, you need to know and understand:**
> - **main external economic changes that can occur**
> - **their impact on different businesses**
> - **government economic objectives and policies**
> - **how these can impact on business decisions.**
>
> 1. What is meant by the 'business cycle'?
> 2. Differentiate between a 'boom' and a 'recession'.
> 3. State **two** possible effects of an increase in GDP on business decisions.

Exam-style questions – Exam-style questions provide you with an opportunity to practice what you have learnt in each topic. They have been written to help prepare you for the types of questions you will face in the examination.

> ## Exam-style questions
>
> ### Paper 1
>
> #### Section A
>
> 1. Explain **two** ways in which a country might benefit from entrepreneurs opening new businesses. **[3]**
> 2. Explain **two** reasons why a business might fail. **[3]**
>
> #### Section B
>
> 3. **a** Analyse the differences between social enterprises and other businesses. **[8]**
>   **b** 'Any hard-working person can become a successful entrepreneur.' Discuss whether you agree with this statement. **[12]**

Improve this answer – This is an opportunity for you to evaluate a sample answer to a given question. Advice and guidance are provided to help you assess the answer and then apply that advice to your own answer in 'Your challenge'.

> ### Improve this answer
>
> This is a student's answer to question 2. Skills are shown in brackets to help you.
>
> Location is important for any business. [K] If the site is too expensive it can mean that costs are too high and no profit is made. [An] Sadiq must have chosen a cheap location.
>
> All new businesses need customers and the quicker customers are gained, the more successful the business is likely to become. [K] Sadiq's customers will pay money to the business and this can then be used to pay the costs of the business and pay back any loans that were needed to set it up. [An]
>
> ### Your challenge
>
> See whether you can improve this answer. It seems to lack the very important 'skill' of application. Just by referring to 'Sadiq' does not make the answer applied. A better answer is given online – but write yours out first!

Research task – A research task is provided at the end of each section, to allow you to put into practice the ideas and skills you have encountered in a bigger task.

> ### Unit 3 Research task – Marketing
>
> #### The Apple success story
>
> Some business analysts describe Apple Inc. as the most successful business in all of history. It was started in 1976. It has grown to become the most valuable company in the world (by market values of its shares). Its brand name and logo are valued more highly than those of any other business. Total global revenue exceeds $250 billion and this figure is much higher than many countries' Gross Domestic Product. Its new product launches – such as that for iPhone 7 – have become international media events. Customers have been known to queue for days outside Apple stores to even have a chance of purchasing the latest newly released product.
>
> As well as operating 478 physical shops in 17 different countries, it also operates the online Apple store and the iTunes Store which is the world's most successful online music retailer. Apple Inc. uses many different forms of promotion but it is increasingly using online methods and social media to communicate with existing and potential consumers. None of these advertisements or social media sites carry details about Apple Inc.'s 'sale prices' or 'special discounts'. Competing with rivals by reducing prices is just not Apple Inc.'s approach.
>
> How can this incredible success be explained?

Unit 1
Business and its environment

1 Enterprise

Learning outcomes

The exercises in this chapter will help you to practise what you have learnt about:

- What is meant by business activity
- Analysing opportunity cost and the economic problem
- How businesses can create value
- Applying the characteristics of successful entrepreneurs
- Analysing why new businesses can fail
- The importance of enterprise and entrepreneurs to a country's economy
- The objectives (triple bottom line) and roles of social enterprises.

KEY TERMS

Consumer goods	Added value
Consumer services	Opportunity cost
Capital goods	Entrepreneur
Factors of production	Social enterprise
Creating value	Triple bottom line

Key skills exercises

Knowledge and understanding

To answer the questions in this chapter, you need to know and understand:

- **nature of business activity**
- **important factors of production**
- **skills and personal qualities needed by successful entrepreneurs**
- **objectives of social enterprises.**

1. List the **four** factors of production.
2. Draw a simple diagram that represents adding or creating value.
3. Define 'opportunity cost'.
4. What is meant by 'the business environment is dynamic'?
5. List **five** characteristics of a successful entrepreneur.
6. List **three** reasons why a recently established business might fail.
7. Give **three** ways in which a country benefits from the start-up of new businesses.
8. List the **three** objectives of most social enterprises.

1 Enterprise

Knowledge, understanding and application

Remember to use the context provided either by the question or the data response material in your answer.

Sami's new business

Sami lives in a low-income country with few job opportunities. He is bored with his job in a petrol service station where he has worked since leaving school. He feels that he is being watched over all the time by his manager. He plans to set up a business with a small sum of money given to him by a relative. He will make and decorate ceramic pots to sell to tourists. Sami started making pots in an Art class at school and enjoyed it. He will use a simple pottery wheel and an electric kiln to 'fire' the pots. He cannot work from home as pottery can be very dusty work. Clay and paint to decorate the pots will be bought from suppliers. He wants to use his skill to make pots for most of the working day. However, he knows that he will have to keep records of all of the transactions his business has with suppliers and customers. He thinks that he will have to employ someone to help him with the selling of the pots and the administration of the business.

TIP
Do not make up your reasons! Read the case study carefully and identify two reasons why Sami took this decision.

9 Explain **two** reasons why Sami decided to set up his own business.

WORKED EXAMPLE

One reason is that Sami wants to be independent by owning his own business. **[K]** This is shown by the fact that 'he feels he is being watched over all the time by his manager' which does not give him any independence at all. **[Ap]**

10 Explain **two** factors of production that Sami will need before he can start operating his business.

11 Explain **two** challenges that Sami will face in starting his business.

12 Explain how Sami will create value in his business.

Knowledge, understanding, application and analysis

The skill of analysis requires that you explain why or how something is a benefit or why or how something could happen.

13 Analyse **two** benefits to Sami's country of his decision to start up his own business.

WORKED EXAMPLE

Sami will employ at least one other worker. **[K]** He will need someone to help him sell pots and carry out the administrative tasks such as looking after the paperwork. **[Ap]** This will help reduce unemployment in Sami's country. **[A]**

14 Analyse **two** reasons why Sami's business could fail.

Cambridge AS and A Level Business

Knowledge, understanding, application, analysis and evaluation

The skill of evaluation requires that you make supported decisions, draw conclusions and give recommendations.

15 Do you think Sami's business will be successful? Justify your answer.

> **TIP**
> For Q15, think about at least one reason why Sami's new business might be successful (e.g. perhaps something to do with his own skills?). Then consider what problems might arise which would impact on the success of Sami's business. Analyse how and why these factors would affect the success of Sami's business and come to an overall and justified conclusion.

16 Discuss the most important entrepreneurial characteristics that Sami will need to help make the business a success.

Exam-style questions

Paper 1

Section A

1 Explain **two** ways in which a country might benefit from entrepreneurs opening new businesses. **[3]**

2 Explain **two** reasons why a business might fail. **[3]**

Section B

3 a Analyse the differences between social enterprises and other businesses. **[8]**

b 'Any hard-working person can become a successful entrepreneur.' Discuss whether you agree with this statement. **[12]**

Paper 2

SPL

Sadiq set up SPL three years ago. The business offers boat and boat engine repair services. Sadiq located his business in a small workshop next to a large harbour. There are many small boats moored in the harbour.

Sadiq is a skilled mechanic and a keen boat owner. He used to work for a large car manufacturer but found the work repetitive. He was able to obtain a bank loan at a low interest rate to provide the capital for his business. He works long hours as he does not employ any workers. He likes dealing with customers directly. He does all of the paperwork for the business.

He belongs to a sailing club and is friends with many of the members. Sadiq buys in boat and engine repair parts for his customers and his final price for each job includes the cost of these parts and the time he has spent on it. He thinks he might be able to further create value by selling new boat engines to customers whose engines cannot be repaired.

Sadiq is very pleased with the performance of his business and he plans to expand it in future.

1   **a**   Define the term 'capital'. **[2]**

    b   Briefly explain the term 'create value'. **[3]**

2   Explain **two** factors, other than Sadiq's own personal qualities, that have led to the success of SPL. **[6]**

3   Analyse how Sadiq's personal qualities have helped the business be successful. **[8]**

4   Evaluate whether Sadiq is right to plan for the future expansion of his business. **[11]**

Improve this answer

This is a student's answer to question 2. Skills are shown in brackets to help you.

> Location is important for any business. [K] If the site is too expensive it can mean that costs are too high and no profit is made. [An] Sadiq must have chosen a cheap location.
>
> All new businesses need customers and the quicker customers are gained, the more successful the business is likely to become. [K] Sadiq's customers will pay money to the business and this can then be used to pay the costs of the business and pay back any loans that were needed to set it up. [An]

Your challenge

See whether you can improve this answer. It seems to lack the very important 'skill' of application. Just by referring to 'Sadiq' does not make the answer applied. A better answer is given online – but write yours out first!

2 Business structure

Learning outcomes

The exercises in this chapter will help you to practise what you have learnt about:

- The three levels of economic activity
- Differentiating between private sector and public sector
- The different forms of legal organisation of businesses and their advantages and disadvantages
- Which form of legal organisation is most appropriate in different circumstances.

KEY TERMS

Primary sector
Secondary sector
Tertiary sector
Private sector
Public sector
Mixed economy
Free-market economy
Command economy
Sole trader
Partnership
Limited liability

Private limited company
Share
Shareholder
Public limited company
Memorandum of Association
Articles of Association
Franchise
Joint venture
Holding company
Public corporation
Cooperative

Key skills exercises

Knowledge and understanding

To answer the questions in this chapter, you need to know and understand:

- **different levels of economic activity**
- **the different sectors of an economy**
- **the main forms of legal organisation.**

1. State **three** industries in the primary sector.
2. State **three** industries in the secondary sector.
3. State **three** industries in the tertiary sector.
4. State **three** types of economic activity that are usually undertaken by the public sector.
5. Are public limited companies in the private sector or the public sector?
6. What is meant by 'limited liability'?
7. If a small sole-trader business expands by employing one worker, is it now a partnership?
8. State **two** benefits that a partnership has over a sole-trader business.

2 Business structure

9 State **two** benefits that a public limited company has over a private limited company.

10 Give **one** advantage and **one** disadvantage to an entrepreneur of setting up a franchise business.

Knowledge, understanding and application

Remember to use the context provided either by the question or the data response material in your answer.

Gill's dresses

Gill is a skilled dressmaker. She makes dresses to her own designs. She used to sell her dresses to clothes shops but she recently decided to sell them only at city centre markets. Selling at these markets takes up a lot of Gill's time. Currently, she works at home but needs additional space for the inventories of materials she has. She also plans to employ a worker who will help her cut material and sell finished dresses at the markets. Gill's old sewing machine keeps breaking down and she needs to replace it. She is worried that her savings might not be enough to pay for a new one.

11 What evidence above suggests that Gill is a sole trader?

12 State **two** benefits to Gill of taking on a business partner.

TIP
For Q12, read your answer carefully – does it make clear references to Gill and/or her business?

WORKED EXAMPLE

Gill is planning to expand her business by buying/renting additional storage space for materials. **[Ap]** This will need finance and Gill may not have enough savings. **[K]**

13 Is Gill's business in the private sector or public sector?

14 In which level of economic activity would you classify Gill's dress-making business?

Knowledge, understanding, application and analysis

The skill of analysis requires that you explain why or how something is a benefit or a disadvantage.

Gill decides to form a partnership with her friend, Maria, who is keen to make dresses but is not very skilled. She has told Gill that she will put a substantial amount of capital into the business and that 'she knows a lot about fashion'.

A specialist clothing retailer has suggested a joint venture proposal to the partners. The owner plans to open a small fashion shop in the city and has asked them to supply dresses. The retailer would manage the sale of the dresses.

15 Analyse **one** disadvantage to Gill of taking on a partner.

16 Analyse **one** benefit and **one** drawback to Gill and her partner of converting the business into a private limited company.

7

Cambridge AS and A Level Business

> **WORKED EXAMPLE**
>
> The benefit would be that both Gill and her partner will have limited liability. **[K]** Her business partner plans to 'put a substantial amount of capital into the business'. **[Ap]** To protect their other assets from being liquidated if the business fails, Gill and her partner would benefit from only risking the capital they invested in the business. **[A]**

> **TIP**
> Your answer to Q16 should provide the basis of your answer to Q17. Include at least one paragraph explaining your decision regarding their potential formation of a private limited company.

Knowledge, understanding, application, analysis and evaluation

The skill of evaluation requires that you make supported decisions, draw conclusions and give recommendations.

17 Do you think that Gill and her partner should form a private limited company? Justify your answer.

18 Recommend to Gill and her partner whether to form a joint venture with the retailer.

Exam-style questions

Paper 1

Section A

1 Explain the difference between primary sector business activity and tertiary sector business activity. **[3]**

2 Explain **two** benefits to an entrepreneur of starting a franchised business **[3]**

> **TIP**
> For Q1, start with a definition of each and then contrast the difference between them.

Section B

3 **a** Analyse the benefits to a sole trader of forming a partnership. **[8]**

   b 'The owners of all private limited companies should consider converting their businesses into pubic limited companies'. Evaluate this view. **[12]**

>
>
> **TIP**
> Notice there are more marks available for the questions in section B than in section A, so expect to write more. Write in clear paragraphs. So, for example, in answering this question you might write five to six paragraphs. In each one, you should explain one key advantage or disadvantage of public limited companies compared to private limited companies. The final paragraphs should explain and justify why owners of a private limited company might or might not consider converting the business to a public limited company. For example, a small family business that wants to keep control has no need for additional capital as the aim of the business is not to grow – so why take the risk of losing control?

Paper 2

Cassy's jewellery

Cassy makes wedding rings for women and men and other items of jewellery. Sajiv is her business partner. Their business is in the private sector. They sell jewellery through the business website. The sold items are posted to customers. Sajiv is responsible for accounts, arranging finance from the bank and buying material supplies. The partners employ two skilled jewellery makers. Sajiv has invested more capital in the business than Cassy. He is thinking of the benefits of limited liability if their partnership is converted into a private limited company.

Both Cassy and Sajiv want new challenges. They could expand their business – called C and S Gems – by employing more workers and renting a large workshop. However, last week they were asked by a large company, MGC, which makes expensive jewellery if they wanted to buy a franchise from the business. The franchise licence would give Cassy and Sajiv the legal right to copy the company's many well-known jewellery designs and sell them through a shop under the company's own name. The cost of the franchise licence is high and C and S Gems would have to be sold to finance this. 'This franchise would give us less risk and a well-known brand name' said Sajiv.

1. **a** Define the term 'private sector'. **[2]**

   b Briefly explain the term 'limited liability'. **[3]**

2. Explain **two** ways in which tertiary sector businesses could help Cassy's business. **[6]**

3. Analyse the problems that Cassy and Sajiv might experience from changing the business from a partnership to a private limited company. **[8]**

4. Evaluate whether Cassy and Sajiv should sell their business and buy the franchise. **[11]**

Improve this answer

This is a student's answer to Q4. Skills are shown in brackets to help you.

A franchise means buying a licence to trade under the name of another business. [K] If this business is well known with a good brand name, it can reduce operating risks. [A]

MGC is a large company and appears to have a good brand name. [Ap] This means Cassy and Sajiv would not have to spend much on advertising as customers will already know about MGC jewellery designs. [A] Risks will be reduced as MGC will have much experience in operating retail stores and will be able to pass this on to Cassy and Sajiv. [A] They are both ambitious and want new challenges. [Ap] Setting up a new shop and making well-known jewellery designs will give them these challenges. [A] The franchise is likely to be very profitable and they will get a good return on their capital.

Your challenge

See whether you can improve this answer. It seems to lack the important skill of 'evaluation', although the final sentence could be used in a conclusion. The student does not give an overall conclusion supported by the analysis shown. A better answer is given online – but write yours out first!

3 Size of business

Learning outcomes

The exercises in this chapter will help you to practise what you have learnt about:

- The different ways of measuring business size
- The impact of small firms on an economy
- The advantages and disadvantages of small and large businesses
- The strengths and weaknesses of family businesses
- Differentiating between internal and external growth.

KEY TERMS

Revenue

Capital employed

Market capitalisation

Market share

Internal growth

Key skills exercises

Knowledge and understanding

To answer the questions in this chapter, you need to know and understand:

- different ways in which business size can be measured
- benefits of small businesses
- compare the advantages of small and large businesses
- the strengths and weaknesses of family businesses.

1 Define the term 'revenue'.
2 What is meant by 'market capitalisation'?
3 How is market share measured?
4 Why might a business with high 'capital employed' have few employees?
5 State **three** benefits to an economy of small businesses.
6 State **three** advantages large businesses often have compared with small businesses.
7 State **three** common strengths of family businesses.
8 State **three** common weaknesses of family businesses.
9 What is meant by the term 'internal growth'?

3 Size of business

Knowledge, understanding and application

Remember to use the context provided either by the question or the data response material in your answer.

RC Enterprises (RCE)

RCE is a retailing business in country X. It sells computers, computing accessories and software to business customers and consumers. This is a competitive market and average prices for computers fell by 5% last year. Last year, RCE's total revenue was $123 million. This is forecasted to rise to $128 million this year. Last year, the sales of all retailers of computers, computing accessories and software in country X totalled $354 million. Other data about this retail market are shown in Table 3.1.

Last year's data for country X	RCE	Retailer A	Retailer B	All other retailers in this market
Capital employed	$100m	$75m	$66m	$35m
Employees	1700	1800	1200	400
Revenue	$123m	$120m	$75m	$36m

Table 3.1

Most of the 'other retailers' shown in Table 3.1 are small, recently established retailers who sell only via the internet not shops. The revenue of these businesses has grown faster than that of the three big retailers in country X over the last two years.

10 Calculate RCE's market share last year.

> **WORKED EXAMPLE**
>
> $$\text{Market share \%} = \frac{\text{Revenue of business}}{\text{Total market sales}} \times 100$$

11 Calculate RCE's forecast market share this year assuming total market sales increase by 10% from last year.

12 Suggest **one** reason why RCE's market share has fallen.

13 Which is the measure of business size that leads to Retailer A being the largest in the market?

14 What percentage of all employees in this retail industry did Retailer A employ last year?

15 Suggest **one** reason why 'other retailers' accounted for 10.2% of market share last year yet only employed 7.8% of total employees in this retail industry.

> **TIP**
>
> For Q11, calculate total market sales this year by adding 10% of last year's total sales to last year's total sales; then use the market share formula using RCE's forecast sales for this year.

Knowledge, understanding, application and analysis

The skill of analysis requires that you explain 'why' or 'how' something is an advantage or a drawback.

16 Analyse **one** advantage to RCE of using the market share measure of size.

17 Analyse **one** benefit and **one** disadvantage to RCE of opening more shops selling computers, accessories and software.

> **WORKED EXAMPLE**
>
> One disadvantage of opening more shops is that it will increase business costs. **[K]** Computers and software are often bought online as most customers for these products will already have online access. **[Ap]** The new shop will mean that RCE's costs will rise but its sales revenue might not and this could lead to a loss being made. **[A]**

TIP
For Q18, think about whether this is the best method to use for measuring size of business in this industry?

Knowledge, understanding, application, analysis and evaluation

The skill of evaluation requires that you make supported decisions, draw conclusions and give recommendations.

18 Do you think that RCE should aim to become the largest business in this retail market by using the 'number of employees' as the measure of size?

19 Do you think that the government of country X should support small retailers in this industry?

Exam-style questions

Paper 1

Section A

1 Explain the difference between internal and external business growth. **[3]**

2 Explain two ways in which the size of businesses in car manufacturing could be measured. **[3]**

Section B

3 **a** Analyse the benefits and drawbacks to a family-owned beauty salon business from expanding by opening more salons. **[8]**

   b 'The government should support only large businesses in the economy as small businesses are much less important.' Evaluate this view. **[12]**

3 Size of business

Paper 2

RT Engineering (RTE)

RTE is a small business that manufactures advanced electric motors for use in washing machines. Although it has a low market share in the market for washing machine components, it supplies two of the largest washing machine manufacturers in country Y. It also exports 10% of its output. RTE designed these motors to be quiet, efficient and very reliable. The private limited company employs 45 workers. The total washing machine industry in country Y, including all suppliers, employs 2,500 workers.

RTE is a family-owned business. Sadiq is the current managing director. The business was started by Sadiq's great grandfather. It has expanded by internal growth. Sadiq only takes ten days holiday each year. He is reluctant to change manufacturing methods. His brother's son, Asif, who is keen to take over as managing director in three years' time when Sadiq plans to retire, wants to introduce the most advanced production processes. Sadiq has thought about recruiting an external manager to help Asif learn about management.

1   **a**   Define the term 'market share'. **[2]**

    b   Briefly explain the term 'small business'. **[3]**

2   Explain **two** advantages to RTE from growing internally. **[6]**

3   Analyse **two** reasons why the government of country Y might choose to support small businesses such as RTE. **[8]**

4   Evaluate the advantages and disadvantages of RTE being a family business. **[11]**

Improve this answer

This is a student's answer to Q3. Skills are shown in brackets to help you.

Firstly, the country benefits from foreign currency from exports. [K] By supporting businesses which export some of their output the country's economy will benefit from more foreign currency. This could be used to buy important imports for the country. [A]

Secondly, small businesses, taken together, employ many people in the whole country. [K] By employing people, the rate of unemployment will fall and the government will have to pay out less in unemployment benefits. [A]

Your challenge

See whether you can improve this answer. It seems to lack the skill of application to the business in the case study. A better answer is given online – but write yours out first!

4 Business objectives

Learning outcomes

The exercises in this chapter will help you to practise what you have learnt about:

- The importance of business objectives and how these are translated into targets
- The importance of objectives being SMART
- The links between mission statement, objectives and strategy
- The role of objectives in decision-making
- How to communicate objectives to stakeholders
- Assessing the reasons why objectives might change over time
- Evaluating the influence of ethics and corporate social responsibility on objectives.

KEY TERMS

Corporate objectives
SMART objectives
Mission statement

Corporate social responsibility (CSR)
Management by Objectives
Ethical code of conduct

Key skills exercises

Knowledge and understanding

To answer the questions in this chapter, you need to know and understand:

- **the importance of setting objectives**
- **the relationship between corporate objectives and strategy**
- **the need to communicate objectives**
- **why objectives might change over time**
- **the increasing importance of corporate social responsibility and ethical decision-making.**

1. State **two** examples of corporate objectives.
2. What do the letters 'SMART' stand for?
3. What are the differences between 'objectives' and 'strategies'?
4. Define the term 'mission statement'.
5. How is the mission statement of a business related to its objectives?
6. Give **one** way in which a business could demonstrate 'corporate social responsibility'.
7. Define 'Management by Objectives'.
8. Give **two** ways in which corporate objectives could be communicated to any one stakeholder group.
9. What is **one** purpose of an 'ethical code' of conduct?

4 Business objectives

Knowledge, understanding and application

Remember to use the context provided either by the question or the data response material in your answer.

> ### JD Traders (JDT)
>
> Jacques is managing director of JDT. The company buys wooden furniture from foreign suppliers and sells it through its retail store. It was set up two years ago. Initially, trading was very difficult and Jacques was mainly focused on the business's survival just selling enough to cover costs. Recently, the growing reputation of the business for good-quality products sold at fair prices has helped sales to rise.
>
> Jacques wants to expand JDT's sales by 10% each year. He plans to open a store in another city next year and employ more workers. The workers would be offered generous employment contracts as Jacques wants excellent customer service to be a key feature of his business. Workers will have more job security than those working for other local businesses.
>
> Jacques has recently rejected an offer by a foreign supplier of 100 wooden tables at very low prices. Jacques believed that the wood had been felled illegally from an ancient forest and that new replacement trees had not been planted.

TIP
You need to read the data response material carefully to be able to answer Q10.

10 How has the corporate objective of this business changed over time?

11 Suggest **one** SMART objective for this business to achieve next year.

12 Suggest **two** ways in which JDT seems to be acting 'socially responsibly'.

WORKED EXAMPLE

One way to act socially responsibly is to treat workers fairly. **[K]** JDT will do this by offering generous employment contracts giving better job security than other local employees. **[Ap]**

13 Suggest a suitable 'mission statement' for JDT.

Knowledge, understanding, application and analysis

The skill of analysis requires that you explain why or how something is an advantage or disadvantage or why or how different aspects of decision-making may impact on others.

14 Analyse **one** advantage to JDT of adopting a system of 'Management by Objectives'.

15 Analyse **two** benefits to JDT of using a decision-making model with clear objectives.

Cambridge AS and A Level Business

> **WORKED EXAMPLE**
>
> The model puts objectives at the centre of decision-making. Decision-making needs a focus or otherwise the decisions will not achieve the required objectives. **[K]** JDT wants to increase sales by 10% each year. **[Ap]** So the plan to open a new shop is appropriate as the new shop should increase sales of furniture. **[A]**

16 Analyse the possible links between the mission statement suggested in your answer to Q12 and the objectives and strategies of JDT.

Knowledge, understanding, application, analysis and evaluation

The skill of evaluation requires that you make supported decisions, draw conclusions and give recommendations.

17 Discuss whether JDT's profits will rise or fall if the business follows a strict ethical code.

> **TIP**
>
> For Q17, think about whether ethical decision-making will add to costs or increase future revenue. You need to give an overall conclusion/judgement that is supported by the arguments that you use.

18 Evaluate the importance of corporate social responsibility to JDT's future success.

> **TIP**
>
> For Q18, explain why CSR might be important to the company's success, but also weigh up other factors that might be important to JDT's overall success.

Exam-style questions

Paper 1

Section A

1 Explain the difference between a mission statement and a corporate objective. **[3]**

2 Explain what an 'ethical business decision' means. **[3]**

Section B

3 **a** Analyse the benefits to business decision-making of having clear objectives. **[8]**

b 'Our business cannot afford to be socially responsible. Our market is so competitive we must aim to achieve the lowest costs possible.' Evaluate this statement. **[12]**

Paper 2

CC Trucks (CCT)

CCT makes trucks for mining companies. The vehicles are huge – and expensive. To encourage mining companies to buy its trucks, CCT offers a range of special offers and services such as long guarantee periods. Recently, a CCT salesperson was found guilty of offering bribes to a mine company executive to sign a large order for CCT trucks. 'Did this salesperson not know about our ethical code?' complained CCT's managing director to the other directors. 'This has left me thinking that perhaps our employees are not fully aware either of this code or of CCT's mission statement and our SMART corporate objective.'

CCT used to be the only major manufacturer of large mining trucks but two Chinese manufacturers have recently entered the market. The global economic slowdown has reduced the demand for mined products such as metals and prices of these are falling.

CCT has a very small number of employees leaving the company each year. The workforce has some of the best working conditions in the secondary sector of industry.

1 **a** Define the term 'ethical code'. **[2]**

   b Briefly explain the term 'SMART objectives'. **[3]**

2 Explain **one** disadvantage to CCT of not communicating objectives clearly. **[6]**

3 Analyse why it might be necessary for CCT to change its objectives over time. **[8]**

4 Evaluate whether ethical decision-making will conflict with CCT's future profitability. **[11]**

Improve this answer

This is a student's answer to Q4. Skills are shown in brackets to help you.

Ethical decisions are those based on a moral code of conduct. [K] This means that the business is trying to do the 'right thing' by not taking bribes, not employing child labour, not using misleading advertisements and so on. [K] Ethical business decision-making can lead to higher costs. [K] For example, using cheap immigrant or child labour and not offering employment contracts can result in very low labour costs. These low costs can either be used to keep prices low or raise profit margins. [A]

Offering bribes can increase the sales revenue of a business. By not offering bribes as company policy, important orders can be lost in countries where this kind of, usually illegal, financial incentive is expected by business people or government officials. [A]

By following an ethical code and using ethics as a basis for decision-making then of course CCT will make lower profits in the future. [E, but not well applied or supported].

Your challenge

See whether you can improve this answer, which is strong on knowledge and analysis. It seems to lack the very important 'skills' of application and evaluation. A better answer is given online – but write yours out first!

5 Stakeholders in a business

Learning outcomes

The exercises in this chapter will help you to practise what you have learnt about:

- Different stakeholder groups – their roles, rights, responsibilities
- How stakeholder objectives can be affected by business decision-making and changes in business objectives
- Why businesses should be accountable to stakeholders
- Understanding, analysing and evaluating potential conflict between stakeholder interests.

KEY TERMS

Stakeholders
Stakeholder concept

Key skills exercises

Knowledge and understanding

To answer the questions in this chapter, you need to know and understand:
- **different types of business stakeholders and their likely objectives**
- **how businesses could make efforts to meet these objectives.**

1. Define the term 'stakeholder'.
2. State **two** likely objectives of employees of a business.
3. Why is government interested in the activities of a business?
4. Why is the local community likely to be affected by the activities of a local business?
5. What rights do customers have?
6. Why is a business's bank interested in the decisions taken by that business?
7. Are shareholders also stakeholders in a limited company?
8. State **one** possible conflict of interest between any two stakeholder groups of a business.
9. Give an example of how a change in business objectives could affect stakeholders.

Knowledge, understanding and application

Remember to use the context provided either by the question or the data response material in your answer.

South Central Trains (SCT)

SCT is a private limited company. It has a seven-year licence from the government to operate trains in one region of country X. It is not making a profit. It has to repay a bank loan next month and it has many suppliers (creditors) who must also be paid. SCT's managers have just announced a large increase in ticket prices. 'As the main road into the capital city will be dug up and widened for the next few months, this is a good opportunity to earn more revenue from train customers. Higher prices will bring more cash into the business too,' said the Managing Director.

SCT has delayed buying new trains and it operates old trains that have high pollution emissions. Some train workers have complained about the impact on their health. 'If we can start to make a profit, we can ask shareholders to invest by buying more shares to help pay for new trains,' explained the Managing Director to other SCT Directors.

10 Why are SCT's creditors interested in the performance of this business?

11 Outline **two** objectives of the bank as one of SCT's stakeholders.

12 Outline **one** conflict of objectives between two of SCT's stakeholders.

WORKED EXAMPLE

SCT operates old trains. This might increase profits for shareholders in the short term as the business does not use profits to buy new trains **[Ap]** – benefiting shareholders as business profits is a major objective for this group. **[K]** However, old trains are polluting **[Ap]** and this is damaging the health of the train workers – who have the objective of a safe and clean working environment. **[K]**

13 Suggest **one** way in which SCT could act responsibly towards the local community.

Knowledge, understanding, application and analysis

The skill of analysis requires that you explain why or how something is a benefit or a drawback or why or how different stakeholder objectives may impact on each other.

14 Analyse **one** advantage to SCT of satisfying stakeholder objectives.

15 Analyse **one** benefit and **one** drawback to SCT of paying the bank and creditors as soon as possible.

> **WORKED EXAMPLE**
>
> One drawback is that paying the bank and creditors quickly will reduce the cash held in the business. **[K]** This cash could have been used by SCT to help buy new trains or stop the existing ones from polluting so much, which would have benefited its workers and the environment. **[Ap/A]**

16 Analyse how the potential conflict identified in the answer to Q12 might be resolved by SCT.

> **WORKED EXAMPLE**
>
> By investing in new trains, using retained profits, which are cleaner and use less fuel **[K/Ap]** the business would improve working conditions and increase future profitability. **[An]**

Knowledge, understanding, application, analysis and evaluation

The skill of analysis requires that you make supported decisions, draw conclusions and give recommendations.

17 Discuss whether SCT should only aim to satisfy shareholders' objectives and not those of other stakeholders.

18 Evaluate the importance of being socially responsible to SCT's future success.

> **TIP**
> For Q17, think about whether shareholders are likely to gain or lose from a long-term policy of not satisfying other stakeholder objectives.

Exam-style questions

Paper 1

Section A

1. Explain the role of creditors and investors in a business. **[3]**
2. Explain what responsibilities customers and the government have to a business. **[3]**

Section B

3. **a** Analyse the objectives of any **two** stakeholder groups in a business. **[8]**
   b 'We cannot possibly meet the objectives of all stakeholder groups so we will only aim to satisfy our shareholders'. Evaluate this statement from the senior manager of a business. **[12]**

5 Stakeholders in a business

Paper 2

DF Farms (DFF)

DFF owns several farms in country Y. It employs temporary workers at busy times of the year and pays low wages as unemployment is high. The farms use many chemicals such as pest controls and weedkillers. These chemical products protect the crops and increase the amount the farms produce. DFF does not know whether these chemicals affect local wildlife or customers who consume these products.

The Chief Executive Officer (CEO) of DFF sent a report to all shareholders recently. The report included: 'We know that stakeholder objectives help determine our business decisions but we need to make a profit too. Social responsibility is all very well, but you, the shareholders, take risks with the capital you invested and our responsibility is to you.'

1 **a** Define the term 'stakeholder objectives'. [2]

 b Explain what 'social responsibility' means. [3]

2 Explain how DFF's objective to make profits affects any one stakeholder group other than shareholders. [6]

3 Analyse how conflict has arisen within DFF between the objectives of different stakeholder groups. [8]

4 Evaluate the factors that could make DFF become more socially responsible. [11]

Improve this answer

This is a student's answer to Q2. Skills are shown in brackets to help you.

A profit objective means making profits for shareholders. They invest in the business and expect a return on their investment. [K] Higher prices can lead to higher profits. This will be good for shareholders but not good for customers who have to pay the higher prices. [A] If they cannot afford higher prices then they will have to buy less. So, by trying to increase profits which benefits shareholders, higher prices will leave customers worse off than before and they suffer from the objective of higher profits. [A]

Your challenge

See whether you can improve this answer, which does show some understanding and analyses a possible impact on customers of a profit objective. It lacks the very important 'skill' of application, however. A better answer is given online – but write yours out first!

6 Business structure (A Level)

Learning outcomes

The exercises in this chapter will help you to practise what you have learnt about:

- Differentiating between local, national and multinational businesses
- The reasons for the growth of international trading links and multinational businesses
- Analysing and evaluating the impact of multinationals on the countries they establish in and the relationships between multinationals and the state
- Arguments for and against privatisation.

KEY TERMS

Free trade
Protectionism
Tariffs
Quotas

Globalisation
Multinational business
Privatisation

Key skills exercises

Knowledge and understanding

To answer the questions in this chapter, you need to know and understand:

- reasons for growth of both international trade and multinational businesses
- the impact – positive and negative – of international trade and multinationals on the countries in which they operate
- relationships between multinational corporations (MNCs) and the states they operate in
- arguments for and against selling state-owned industries to the private sector.

1 List **two** reasons for the growth in the number of multinational corporations.
2 List **three** benefits of the growth of international trade links.
3 List **three** possible limitations to a business from the growth of international trade links.
4 Define 'free trade'.
5 Define 'protectionism'.
6 Outline the main difference between 'local' businesses and 'national' businesses.
7 Outline the main difference between 'national' businesses and 'multinationals'.
8 List **three** multinational businesses that operate in your country.
9 List **three** possible benefits to a country of having multinational businesses operating there.
10 State **one** possible advantage and **one** possible disadvantage of the privatisation of a country's state owned electricity industry.

6 Business structure (A Level)

Knowledge, understanding and application

Remember to use the context provided either by the question or the data response material in your answer.

Arav Telecom Company (ATC)

ATC was started by Arav 12 years ago. It specialises in installing internet and satellite communication systems into homes and offices. Most of these systems are imported. Arav wants to expand the business into becoming an internet service provider. However, in country X, where, ATC operates, this operation is legally controlled by the state owned telecoms business StatCom.

ATC used to operate from one location in the southern region but it has now opened bases in other parts of the country too. It has a high market share but further expansion is limited by the challenging economic conditions in country X. Arav and his senior managers are considering starting internet and satellite installation operations in other countries such as country Y. This would have been impossible until recently, but last year country X became part of a large free trade area with six other countries. Most of these countries lack good internet and satellite communication systems.

StatCom has a legal monopoly on all phone lines in country X and is the only internet service provider. The government is in debt and is planning to sell StatCom to the private sector. At the same time, it will allow other businesses to operate phone lines and provide internet services. The existing managers of StatCom believe that, despite the privatisation, the business will remain the largest telecommunications provider in country X for many years. Many StatCom workers and suppliers are opposed to this privatisation but customer groups and potential competitor companies have expressed support for the government's decision.

11 Would you describe ATC as being a local or a national business? Outline the reason for your answer.

> **WORKED EXAMPLE**
>
> ATC used to be a local business operating 'from one location'. **[K/Ap]** It is now a national business as 'it has opened other bases in other parts of the country too'. **[K/Ap]**

12 Explain why ATC's senior management is considering operating in other countries.

13 Would ATC experience any problems in operating in other countries? Explain your answer.

14 How could ATC be affected by country X increasing international trade links with other countries?

> **TIP**
> Refer to information in the data response material – perhaps by quoting from it – in support of your answer to Q12.

Knowledge, understanding, application and analysis

The skill of analysis requires that you explain why or how something is an advantage or a disadvantage or why or how different elements may affect or impact on each other.

15 Analyse the possible advantages to **two** stakeholders in StatCom of its privatisation.

16 Analyse the possible disadvantages to **two** other stakeholder groups in StatCom of its privatisation.

17 Explain **two** ways in which businesses in country Y might be affected by ATC's decision to expand operations in that country.

23

> **WORKED EXAMPLE**
>
> One way other businesses will be affected is increased competition if these businesses are in the internet/satellite installation industry. **[K/Ap]**. The existing businesses installing internet/satellite connections will now have a new competitor and ATC might offer lower prices to customers to get established in the new country. This could make existing businesses lower their prices too, reducing their profits margins. **[A]**

18 Analyse the other possible impacts on country Y from ATC's decision to expand there.

Knowledge, understanding, application, analysis and evaluation

The skill of evaluation requires that you make supported decisions, draw conclusions and give recommendations.

19 Discuss whether ATC should become a multinational business.

20 Evaluate the government's decision to privatise StatCom.

> **TIP**
> For Q19, think about the costs and risks of such a decision and compare these with the potential opportunities.

Exam-style questions

Paper 3

> **State Energy Company (SEC)**
>
> SEC is a public corporation in country Z. It is the only supplier of energy to businesses and households in this country. SEC is legally required to follow strict rules about using low-pollution sustainable methods of producing energy. Workers in SEC are well paid and have good job security. SEC is currently not profitable despite customers complaining about high prices.
>
> The government has given SEC's senior managers the objective of making a profit. They plan to achieve this by expanding the corporation's energy operations into another country – Y. This country has many small competing energy suppliers and two loss-making energy companies failed last year, making all their workers redundant. Electricity prices are very high. SEC managers plan to take over several of these small energy providers in country Y and start to dominate the market there.
>
> A new government has just been elected in country Z. It has decided to privatise SEC and allow the entry of competing energy companies in the market for electricity.

1 Analyse the likely impact on country Y from SECs decision to set up operations in this country. **[10]**

2 Discuss the potential impact on SEC's stakeholders of the decision by the government to privatise the business. **[14]**

6 Business structure (A Level)

Improve this answer

This is a student's answer to Q2. Skills are shown in brackets to help you.

Privatisation means selling a state-owned business to the private sector. Governments can sell to the private sector state-owned businesses when they are short of money or when they believe that a competing free market works better than a state-operated monopoly. [K]

SEC's workers will not want the privatisation to go ahead. They might lose their good pay level [Ap] and secure jobs as a privatised energy business will focus on raising profits perhaps at the expense of workers. [A]

Customers might also lose out as the privatised business will want to turn a loss into a profit to give a return to investors. [K] The decision might be made to increase energy prices even further. As there are no really close substitutes for electricity in the home or in factories, customers will have to pay the higher prices. [Ap/A]

The local community and environmental pressure groups might also lose as the privatised business will probably make cost-cutting a priority not the environment. [K] It might be more expensive to use non-polluting sustainable energy methods than just burning oil or coal. So a privatised SEC might damage the environment and put people's health at risk. [Ap/A]

Your challenge

See whether you can improve this answer, which identifies three relevant stakeholders, focuses on energy issues and analyses possible impacts on stakeholders. However, it seems to lack a very important 'skill' – evaluation. There are no 'counter-arguments' or advantages mentioned at all and there is no overall conclusion. A better answer is given online – but write yours out first!

7 Size of business (A Level)

Learning outcomes

The exercises in this chapter will help you to practise what you have learnt about:

- The different forms of external growth
- Assessing the impact of external growth on business stakeholders
- The reasons why external growth might not achieve original objectives
- Joint ventures and strategic alliances (see also Chapter 2 for joint ventures)
- Problems resulting from rapid growth.

KEY TERMS

External growth	Vertical integration – forward
Merger	Vertical integration – backward
Takeover	Conglomerate integration
Synergy	Strategic alliance
Horizontal integration	

Key skills exercises

Knowledge and understanding

To answer the questions in this chapter, you need to know and understand:

- types of external growth
- the different impact these can have on stakeholder groups
- reasons for the use of joint ventures and strategic alliances
- how business deals with the problems of rapid business growth.

1. Explain the difference between internal and external business growth.
2. Explain the difference between a merger and a takeover.
3. Explain the difference between horizontal and vertical integration.
4. Explain the difference between forward vertical integration and backward vertical integration.
5. Explain what 'conglomerate integration' means.
6. Explain what 'synergy' means.
7. Suggest **two** problems that could result from rapid business growth.

7 Size of business (A Level)

Knowledge, understanding and application

Remember to use the context provided either by the question or the data response material in your answer.

> **Freya's Transport (FT)**
>
> Freya is the majority shareholder and managing director of FT. It is a transport company that operates bus routes throughout the country. It owns 445 buses and has a large route network. A recent survey of FT's bus passengers concluded that the majority thought that 'FT offered excellent service at reasonable fare levels'.
>
> Freya and the other directors have pursued a growth strategy for several years. FT has recently signed an agreement with Company A to to combine this business and its buses and routes into the FT network. Company A is a long-established family-owned business and the family have decided to reduce the management role they undertake. Most workers consider that they are treated like 'family members' and very few leave the business. Some of Company A's routes are the same as FT's and the two businesses used to compete fiercely. Freya has to decide whether to reduce the total number of buses operating on these routes following the integration. She aims to use this integration to make FT much more profitable.
>
> Last year FT bought out a specialist bus manufacturing business, Company B. It supplies FT and other bus operating companies with the large vehicles needed. FT's managers wanted more control over the design and price of this major resource. They have set the objective that newly designed buses will be introduced in 12 months' time. The new designs should make more provision for elderly passengers as many of FT's customers are in the 60+ age group. This integration will give FT's directors control over a manufacturing business for the first time.

TIP
For Q8, use examples from the data response material to illustrate your answer.

8 Is FT using internal or external growth in order to expand?
9 Was the integration with Company A an example of a merger or takeover?
10 Was the integration with Company B an example of a merger or a takeover?
11 Classify the **two** examples of integration explained in the data response material as horizontal, vertical forward or backward, or conglomerate.

> **WORKED EXAMPLE**
>
> When FT bought out a bus manufacturing business this was an example of backward vertical integration because the bus manufacturer is a supplier to FT. **[K/Ap]**

12 Explain **two** possible problems that FT might experience from rapid growth.
13 State **two** ways in which FT's customers might be affected by the integration with Company A.
14 State **two** ways in which FT's customers might be affected by the integration with Company B.

Knowledge, understanding, application and analysis

The skill of analysis requires that you explain why or how something is an advantage or disadvantage or why or how different elements may affect or impact on each other.

15 Analyse the possible advantages to any **two** of FT's stakeholder groups from the integration with Company A.

16 Analyse the possible disadvantages to any **two** of FT's stakeholder groups from the integration with Company B.

17 Analyse **two** likely reasons why FT's managers integrated the business with Company A.

18 Analyse **two** likely reasons why FT's managers integrated the business with Company B.

> **WORKED EXAMPLE**
>
> One reason is this backward vertical integration will ensure a supply of buses to FT in future. **[K/Ap]** It will mean that FT can control the manufacture of buses to its own design and it can obtain the buses more cheaply than if it were buying them from an independent manufacturer. **[A]**

19 Analyse why the original objectives of these forms of integration might not be achieved.

Knowledge, understanding, application, analysis and evaluation

The skill of evaluation requires that you make supported decisions, draw conclusions and give recommendations.

20 Discuss whether FT should continue to expand by using horizontal integration.

21 Evaluate whether FT should expand by vertical integration in future.

TIP
For Q20, consider the potential business drawbacks of such a decision and compare these with the potential opportunities.

Exam-style questions

Paper 3

Chang's Computers (CC)

CC is one of the largest manufacturers of computers and tablets in the region. It was set up by Eddie Chang 15 years ago in his garden workshop. With dedication and creativity, he has expanded the business by buying larger premises three times since the business was set up. It now employs 1,500 workers and produces 200,000 units each year – all sold to retailers in country X. Eddie now plans to start exporting to country Y for the first time. He has discussed forming a joint venture with World Markets Limited (WML). This company has much experience of transporting, promotion and selling electronic equipment in many world markets. It would share the costs of exporting CC's products in country Y but its managers want control over marketing decisions and 60% of the venture's profits.

Eddie and the other CC directors believe that further expansion of the business should come from rapid external growth. 'The computer market is now so competitive that we must achieve larger-scale operations quickly. We could also consider buying computer component makers to give us exclusive access to cutting-edge microchips and other components we need. I would also like to research the possibility of establishing our own chain of CC retail stores to offer customers a dedicated one-stop shop for all of their CC requirements,' reported Eddie at a recent Board meeting.

7 Size of business (A Level)

1. Analyse **one** likely benefit and **one** likely disadvantage to CC of the proposed joint venture. **[10]**
2. Discuss the potential impact on CC's stakeholders of the decision by its management to use rapid external growth to expand the business. **[14]**

Improve this answer

This is a student's answer to Q1. Skills are shown in brackets to help you.

A joint venture exists when two businesses agree to put in capital and management resources to operate a new business opportunity. It is not a merger or a takeover. This joint venture would be between a manufacturer (CC) and a marketing business (WML). [K/Ap]

It would allow CC to concentrate on making the computers and tablets as efficiently as possible and not worry about selling them in another country. [K/Ap]

One disadvantage is that WML will control marketing in country Y and take 60% of the profit. This would leave less profit for CC. [A]

Your challenge

See whether you can improve this answer, which is very brief and lacks detailed application and analysis. A better answer is given online – but write yours out first!

(A Level only)

Learning outcomes

The exercises in this chapter will help you to practise what you have learnt about:

- Why the state intervenes in business activities
- Legal influences on business activity
- The impact of technology on business activities
- Social changes and their impact on business activities
- How the environment and environmental protection influence business activity
- How business strategies can be used to respond to external influences.

KEY TERMS

Monopoly
Social audit
Environmental audit
Information technology
Innovation

Computer aided design (AS Level Operations Management too)
Computer aided manufacturing (AS Level Operations Management too)
Pressure group

Key skills exercises

Knowledge and understanding

To answer the questions in this chapter, you need to know and understand the external influences that can have an impact on business activities, decisions and strategies – legal, technological, social and environmental.

1. State **two** legal controls that, in your own country, impact on how businesses manage their workers.
2. State **two** legal controls that, in your own country, impact on how businesses market their products.
3. State **two** legal controls that, in your own country, impact on the production operations of businesses (e.g. location, disposal of waste).
4. List **four** ways in which new technology can influence business activities/operations.
5. State **two** social changes that could have an impact on business marketing decisions.
6. List **two** reasons why a business might decide to protect the environment.
7. What is the difference between an environmental audit and a social audit?

8 External influences on business activity (A Level only)

Knowledge, understanding and application

Remember to use the context provided either by the question or the data response material in your answer.

> **Timber Products Limited (TP)**
>
> TP manufactures and sells furniture. The timber (cut wood) it uses comes from the large forests that the company owns. Most of the furniture is sold through the company's own retail shops but lower-quality and damaged items are sold directly from the factory with no guarantees. Often these are promoted to customers who visit the factory as being 'same high quality but lower prices'. The forests that TP owns are so large that the company does not replace the trees it cuts down with young trees. This strategy has been recently criticised by a large environmental pressure group as it is not sustainable in the long term. Also, during heavy storms, earth is washed into rivers from the deforested areas and this is making fishing more difficult for local people.
>
> TP finds it difficult to recruit enough workers. It pays low wages to timber cutters and they have dangerous equipment to handle. This recruitment problem is made worse by the country having an ageing population with net immigration falling to low levels last year. These demographic and social changes are also having an impact on the styles of furniture that TP produce.
>
> The government is introducing new legal controls over business activities. A minimum wage is being introduced and strict health and safety regulations at work. Consumer protection is being improved with controls over unfair advertising and poor-quality products.
>
> A new Managing Director has recently been appointed at TP. She wants to make TP a more responsible organisation yet some shareholders oppose this. She wants to buy high technology equipment that is both safer and more adaptable than existing labour controlled machines. They will allow different styles and sizes of furniture to be made by the same computer-controlled equipment.

8 How is TP likely to be affected by the new government legal controls?

9 Outline **two** ways in which new technology might benefit TP?

> **WORKED EXAMPLE**
>
> One benefit of new technology equipment is that it should be safer than the dangerous equipment used now. **[K]** New cutting machines which automatically stop when the operator lets go of it will improve safety in the forests. **[Ap]**

10 How might social and demographic changes affect TP?

11 What action could the pressure group take against TP?

Knowledge, understanding, application and analysis

The skill of analysis requires that you explain why or how something is an advantage or disadvantage or why or how different elements may affect or impact on each other. Remember to apply your answer clearly to the business in the case study.

12 Analyse **two** possible impacts on TP's operations of the proposed legal controls.

13 Analyse **two** ways in which TP could respond to these new legal controls.

Cambridge AS and A Level Business

14 Explain **two** possible disadvantages to TP of adopting new technology.

15 Analyse **two** possible benefits to TP of accepting its responsibility to the environment.

> **WORKED EXAMPLE**
>
> One benefit would be good supply of timber in future if TP replaced cut down trees with newly planted ones. **[K/Ap]** The forests are so large that TP does not bother to plant new trees to replace those cut down. This can cause soil erosion problems that damage the environment. By planting new trees TP will benefit the environment as well as increasing its supply of timber for the future. **[A]**

> **TIP**
> For Q16 explain the costs and possible benefits these controls might have on TP – will costs outweigh benefits for TP?

Knowledge, understanding, application, analysis and evaluation

The skill of evaluation requires that you make supported decisions, draw conclusions and give recommendations.

16 Discuss whether government controls will have a positive or negative impact on TP's future.

17 Evaluate how TP should react to the changing external influences.

Exam-style questions

Paper 3

Bernadette's Meals (BM)

BM produces high-quality prepared foods which are sold in upmarket grocery retailers. BM's food is prepared and packaged, ready for consumers to heat up and serve. All meals are cooked in BM's small kitchen by skilled workers who prepare food by hand, cook it in small quantities using BM's own recipes and package it carefully in attractive microwavable boxes. This old-fashioned production method suits the workers and the management.

The family-owned business has always put quality before market share, but the directors are becoming increasingly concerned about falls in sales and profits over recent years.

BM produces traditional products using old-fashioned recipes that often appeal to older consumers. The population of the country where BM is based is youthful and has been boosted in recent years by large numbers of migrants who have introduced their own food tastes and methods of cooking. As a result, consumer food tastes are changing.

BM's costs are likely to increase as the government has announced that health and safety regulations at work, which used to apply only to large businesses, will now have to be adopted by all businesses. New legal controls on limiting how many days fresh foods can be stored will also affect BM as none of its products are designed to be frozen.

One of BM's directors wants to reduce labour costs and widen the range of foods being produced. These aims would be achieved by purchasing new technology food-processing equipment that can mix food ingredients to many different recipes, portion the food into the right quantities and package the meals automatically.

8 External influences on business activity (A Level only)

1 Analyse **three** problems that BM is likely to experience from introducing technological change. **[10]**

2 Discuss the ways in which BM could respond to changing external influences. **[14]**

Improve this answer

This is a student's answer to Q1. Skills are shown in brackets to help you.

Technological change is being introduced in many industries. It often involves the use of computer-controlled equipment which aids either the design or the manufacturing process. [K] One problem with introducing new technology is it can be very expensive. [K] Many businesses can find it difficult to finance it. If finance is borrowed then this adds to interest costs for several years which will reduce the profits of the business. [A]

The second problem is the resistance of the workforce and – sometimes – management to technological change. [K] It can lead to job losses as it is often more efficient. Workers who remain will need new skills and training. This can be expensive and workers might worry about whether they are able to learn the skills. [A] Managers might be worried about not understanding the new machines too.

Thirdly, new technology can change the way the product is made. This can mean that 'handmade' products are no longer made using traditional methods or materials. [K] This can have a negative impact on consumers who might only have bought the products originally because of the traditional methods of manufacture which can help to give a product a quality image. [A]

Your challenge

See whether you can improve this answer, which clearly lacks any direct application to the business. No evaluation is required as the command word was 'analyse'. A better answer is given online – but write yours out first!

business behaviour (A Level only)

Learning outcomes

The exercises in this chapter will help you to practise what you have learnt about:

- Government economic objectives
- The economic growth and business cycle – and the impact on business and future business strategies
- The causes and business consequences of unemployment
- The causes and business consequences of inflation and deflation
- The business impact of government economic policies used to achieve objectives
- The business impact of tax changes, interest rates and exchange rates
- The causes of market failure
- Government intervention in industry.

KEY TERMS

Economic growth	Exchange rate
Gross Domestic Product (GDP)	Exchange rate depreciation
Business investment	Exchange rate appreciation
Business cycle	Imports
Recession	Exports
Inflation	Fiscal policy
Deflation	Government budget deficit
Working population	Government budget surplus
Unemployment	Monetary policy
Cyclical unemployment	Market failure
Structural unemployment	External costs
Frictional unemployment	Income elasticity of demand
Balance of Payments (current account)	

Key skills exercises

Knowledge and understanding

To answer the questions in this chapter, you need to know and understand:

- main external economic changes that can occur
- their impact on different businesses
- government economic objectives and policies
- how these can impact on business decisions.

1 What is meant by the 'business cycle'?

2 Differentiate between a 'boom' and a 'recession'.

3 State **two** possible effects of an increase in GDP on business decisions.

9 External economic influences on business behaviour (A Level only)

4 Differentiate between 'inflation' and 'deflation'.

5 State **two** economic objectives of most governments.

6 Give **two** ways in which a business might be affected by increased unemployment.

7 Differentiate between an exchange rate appreciation and an exchange rate depreciation.

8 State **two** types of taxes used by most governments to raise revenue.

9 What is meant by 'monetary policy'?

10 What does an income elasticity of '+3' mean?

Knowledge, understanding and application

Remember to use the context provided either by the question or the data response material in your answer.

Exclusive Hotels (EH)

EH is a public limited company. It operates six luxury hotels in country X. High prices are charged for both bedrooms and restaurant meals. Most customers are from country X and only 8% are from other countries – foreign business people and tourists. EH imports most of the food and drinks sold through its hotel restaurants as well as all of the furniture for the hotels' bedrooms.

Recent economic data for country X show that inflation is rising and that unemployment is falling quickly. The government is so worried about higher prices that it has been encouraging the Central Bank to raise interest rates. Yesterday, the Central Bank increased interest rates to 6% and the exchange rate of country X's currency appreciated immediately. The government has also used fiscal policy to reduce demand in the economy. Income tax rates have been increased and the sales tax (VAT) has been raised by 5%. The Chief Executive of EH is worried about the impact on EH of these changes. She told other directors: 'I remember how badly our business was affected by the last recession seven years ago. If the economy goes into recession again, it will damage our type of business in particular.'

11 What stage of the business cycle does country X's economy seem to be in?

12 State **two** ways in which EH could be affected by the increase in interest rates.

13 Which economic objective does the government seem to be aiming to achieve by its fiscal policy changes?

14 State **two** ways in which EH could be affected by the change in the exchange rate.

WORKED EXAMPLE

An appreciation of the currency will make imported food and drink cheaper. **[K/Ap]**

Knowledge, understanding, application and analysis

The skill of analysis requires that you explain why or how something occurs or why or how something is an advantage or disadvantage. Remember to apply your answer clearly to the business in the case study.

15 Analyse why the demand for EH's services fell sharply when the economy was in recession.

16 Analyse how EH could be affected by increasing inflation.

17 Analyse how businesses in country X might be affected by a falling rate of unemployment.

18 Analyse one advantage to EH of economic growth.

> **WORKED EXAMPLE**
>
> One benefit of economic growth to EH is that it often leads to increases in consumer incomes. **[K]** As hotels and catering are usually an income elastic product **[Ap]** any increase in consumer incomes is likely to lead to an even greater relative change in demand for these products. Increased demand will result in higher revenue for EH and higher profit. **[A]**

TIP
For Q19, analyse how changes in rates of tax and interest will impact on EH and assess how the business could respond e.g. build some hotels with fewer facilities and lower prices?

Knowledge, understanding, application, analysis and evaluation

The skill of evaluation requires that you make supported decisions, draw conclusions and give recommendations. To be effective, your judgement must be based upon the business situation in the case study.

19 Discuss how EH could respond to the economic policy decisions taken by the government and the Central Bank.

20 Evaluate the measures EH's managers could take to make the company less affected by the business cycle in country X.

9 External economic influences on business behaviour (A Level only)

Exam-style questions

Paper 3

Bikes For All (BFA)

BFA manufactures bicycles in country Y. There are four models in its product range. The basic shopping model has a retail price of $100. The cross-country model is priced at $150. A racing bicycle model is priced at $350 as it is made from expensive lightweight materials. It has an excellent reputation with serious and professional cyclists. The latest model is an 'e-bike' which uses an advanced battery system, developed and produced by a foreign business, to aid the rider. The retail price for this bicycle is $500. It is the only bicycle model currently exported by BFA and this bicycle accounts for 30% of total output. 25% of the materials and components the company uses are imported.

The economy of country Y is forecast not to grow in 2020. This is largely because the global economy is slowing down and may even be in recession in two years' time, according to some Economists. In addition, country Y's government is using fiscal policy to reduce its huge budget deficit. It has increased taxes and reduced government spending and it is forecast to follow this policy for the next two years. Table 9.1 shows measures of economic performance for Country Y.

	2018	2019 (forecast)	2020 (forecast)
GDP growth rate [%]	3	2	0
Unemployment rate [%]	6	7	9
Inflation [%]	4	3	1
Exchange rate index	100	95	90
Central Bank interest rate [%]	7	6	4

Table 9.1

1 Analyse how BFA could be affected by any **two** of the measures of economic performance (including the forecasted data). **[10]**

2 Recommend how BFA should respond to the economic data for country Y. Justify your recommendation. **[14]**

Improve this answer

This is a student's answer to Q2. Skills are shown in brackets to help you.

BFA is going to be greatly affected by these changes in the external economic environment – if the forecasts turn out to be true. As country Y's economy is forecast not to expand in 2020, the consumer incomes will not be growing. [K] As there is forecast to still be inflation by then, real incomes could fall. [K/A] A depreciating exchange rate will make imported components more expensive and these could reduce BFA profits. [Ap/A] Higher taxes will also reduce consumers' disposable income. [K] With all of these changes in the external economic environment it will be important for BFA to respond quickly.

Firstly, the company could expand production of its cheaper bicycles as these are likely to have a lower income elasticity of demand than the two more expensive models. [Ap] They might be 'inferior' goods, certainly compared to cars which many consumers might not now be able to afford. If demand for the two cheaper models increases then BFA could move resources from making the e-bike and the racing model to the two cheaper designs. [Ap/A]

However, the profit per bicycle could be much less with these two models and BFA might have planned to develop its brand image more effectively in the higher priced segments of the market. [Ap/E]

BFA could start exporting all of the other three designs that it currently does not sell abroad. Other country's economies might not be at risk of recession as that of country Y appears to be. [K] Demand for bicycles might be high and BFA could replace some lost sales in country Y with these new markets. [Ap] A depreciating currency will also make BFA bicycles cheaper abroad so output might not have to be reduced and jobs could be saved. [A] However, BFA would have to be aware of any differences in consumer protection rules between these countries and country Y as well as different laws about bicycle construction and safety. [E]

Your challenge

This answer has some very good points. However, there is no overall evaluated recommendation. See whether you can supply this. A better conclusion is given online – but write yours out first!

Unit 1 Research task – Enterprise

Mydala – an entrepreneur's success

Anisha Singh is one of India's most successful female entrepreneurs. She is the co-founder of MyDala. It is a marketing platform that helps all businesses, especially local businesses, market themselves via social media, mobile and websites. The company helps businesses build brand awareness and drive customers to them. Local businesses as well as online companies are able to reach their right consumer group using Mydala's various platforms. She first identified the market for MyDala after studying the development of coupon style marketing in China.

MyDala is now the largest mobile coupon provider in India, with over 150,000+ retail businesses having used it as a platform nationwide. It was not easy to start up MyDala as investors were originally reluctant to put money into such a new IT-based marketing idea.

Anisha has said: 'From outside it all looks rosy but that definitely wasn't the case for a long time. We just were a determined bunch who weren't ready to hang our hats. There was a time when things were extremely rough for us but we chose to keep innovating till we hit the right formula for exponential growth. Not quitting is what makes MyDala what it is today!'

So what is the secret to her success? 'The best team ever, a lot of hard work and the fact that we ran a business like a business… we had our sights first on profits and then on external funding,' she says. 'We still have our original founding team intact … that is how well we gelled together. I think this made all the difference, to have people who understand, support and encourage one another. Every single member of the team has worked tirelessly through the years. We've all just given our best to the company and it shows.'

Anisha has a clear vision and sense of focus for her business. 'My vision is to see MyDala as the number 1 provider of coupons and loyalty programs with the most extensive merchant base. I foresee that every single Indian will go on MyDala first when they want to shop for food, travel or anything else! We already have a presence in 196 cities and over 100,000 merchants.'

Adapted from openthemagazine.com

Write a report about the work of two entrepreneurs in your own country – one male and one female. Include in your report details of what their businesses do, how they had the original idea for the business and what qualities the entrepreneurs have to help make the businesses successful.

Unit 2
People in organisations

10 Management and leadership

Learning outcomes

The exercises in this chapter will help you to practise what you have learnt about:

- The functions of management
- The importance of good management
- Differentiating between McGregor's Theory X and Y
- Different management/leadership styles
- Assessing the appropriateness of these styles to different business situations
- The iImportance of emotional intelligence.

KEY TERMS

Manager
Leadership
Autocratic leadership
Democratic leadership
Paternalistic leadership

Laissez-faire leadership
Informal leader
Emotional intelligence (EI)
McGregor's Theory X and Theory Y

Key skills exercises

Knowledge and understanding

To answer the questions in this chapter, you need to know and understand:

- **main functions of management**
- **Mintzberg's management roles**
- **main styles of leadership**
- **emotional intelligence.**

1 Explain the difference between a manager and a leader.
2 Explain **two** functions of management.
3 State the **three** management roles identified by Mintzberg.
4 State the **three** features of a manager's 'Interpersonal roles' as suggested by Mintzberg.
5 Define 'autocratic leadership'.
6 Differentiate between 'democratic leadership' and 'laissez-faire' leadership styles.
7 Differentiate between the work typically performed by a manager and work performed by a supervisor.
8 State **two** beliefs of 'Theory X' managers.
9 State **two** beliefs of 'Theory Y' managers.
10 Define 'emotional intelligence'.

Knowledge, understanding and application

Remember to use the context provided either by the question or the data response material in your answer.

Asian Retailers (AR)

AR is a large business with retail stores in several Asian countries. The stores sell clothing, furniture and electrical goods. Fred is the Chief Executive Officer. He was appointed last year after the previous CEO was replaced following shareholder opposition. The owners of AR are very worried about falling sales and profits.

Fred is proud of his reputation as a manager and leader who 'gets things done' and 'stands for no nonsense'. Fred wants to cut costs at AR. He has told all store managers to stop holding weekly meetings with workers to discuss store-related issues. 'Workers should be on the shop floor selling. Managers are paid to think and take key decisions' he said at a recent meeting of all store managers.

Fred has visited nearly all of the AR stores since being appointed. He has reallocated resources from store redecoration to advertising and promotion. He has made sure that pricing and product decisions are coordinated between stores in all countries. He has set all store managers ambitious targets for sales increases. Directors who fail to meet targets for their departments will have their contracts terminated although Fred will leave this to the Human Resources department as he avoids undertaking this type of communication himself.

A major development within AR has been Fred's announcement that all of AR's products will also be made available online through e-commerce. This will need careful planning and a new e-commerce director has been appointed. Fred will report on this and other developments to shareholders at a special General Meeting.

A recent fire in one AR store resulted in very quick decisions by the store manager about an alternative temporary location and how customers' existing orders were to be met. When Fred heard of this he said, 'I told you that my style of leadership always works best.'

11 Which leadership style does Fred seem to be using?

12 Identify **two** management functions undertaken by Fred.

> **WORKED EXAMPLE**
>
> Fred 'sets objectives and targets' and this is a function of management. **[K]**. The case states that Fred has set all store managers ambitious targets for sales increases. **[Ap]**

13 Which of Mintzberg's management roles did Fred seem to be undertaking when he considered the e-commerce option?

14 Outline **two** possible benefits to AR if Fred had adopted the democratic style of leadership.

Knowledge, understanding, application and analysis

The skill of analysis requires that you explain why or how something is important or is an advantage or disadvantage.

15 Analyse why effective leadership is important to AR.

16 Analyse **two** disadvantages of the leadership style that Fred seems to be using.

> **WORKED EXAMPLE**
>
> Fred seems to be using an autocratic style of leadership. **[K]** He 'stands for no nonsense' and cancelled weekly meetings with shop staff which was an opportunity for them to participate. **[Ap]**. This means that he will not get the benefit of the workers' opinions on, for example, what customers seem to most want to buy which could lead to poor decisions about items sold in the shops. **[A]**.

17 Analyse how **two** of Mintzberg's 'Informational roles' are important to effective management of AR.

Knowledge, understanding, application, analysis and evaluation

The skill of evaluation requires that you make supported decisions, draw conclusions and give recommendations. Remember to apply your answers to the case study business. This will greatly increase the relevance of the judgement and evaluation you give.

18 Discuss whether AR's managers should adopt different leadership styles in different situations.

19 Evaluate the importance of EI competencies to good management within AR.

> **TIP**
> For Q18, think about at least three different business situations for AR such as a flood at the warehouse. Explain which leadership style would be most suitable in each case.

Exam-style questions

Paper 1

Section A

1 Outline **two** of Goleman's emotional intelligence competencies. **[5]**

2 Differentiate between 'autocratic leadership' and 'laissez-faire' leadership. **[3]**

Section B

3 Discuss whether the democratic leadership style is ever the most appropriate one to use in business. **[20]**

Paper 2

Rapid Pizza (RP)

RP operates a pizza delivery service. It is owned and managed by Mohamed. The business has a lot of competition and sales have not increased for months. Some workers have recently asked for a pay rise that keeps up with inflation. Mohamed rejected this and said they could all have one free pizza a week instead.

Mohamed studied Business at school and believes that he is an effective manager. 'I am good at telling my workers what to do. I make sure that the business has sufficient resources – capital and labour, in particular – and I think setting targets is really important. Only last week I told my workers that they had to increase sales by 10% next month.' Mohamed has heard of Mintzberg and thinks he undertakes all of the 'management roles' identified by Mintzberg very effectively.

Mohamed likes managing the business but does not like dealing with workers. He gets angry quite quickly – with both customers who complain and with workers who 'try to tell me how to run my business such as which toppings we should have on our pizzas'. He admitted to a friend that he could not understand why his workers did not have the same motivation that he had. He told his friend, 'I do not let them worry about taking decisions as I do that for them. For example, when delivering to a new address I always tell them which route they must take.'

1 **a** Define 'manager'. [2]

   b Briefly explain the term 'management roles'. [3]

2 Explain **two** examples of where Mohamed seems to use autocratic leadership. [6]

3 Analyse the benefits to RP if Mohamed had more emotional intelligence. [8]

4 Discuss the most suitable leadership style to be used within RP. [11]

Improve this answer

This is a student's answer to question 4. Skills are shown in brackets to help you.

> Mohamed seems to use the autocratic style as he tells workers rather than asking them (democratic style) or letting them get on with work themselves (laissez-faire). [K]
>
> If he used the democratic style he could benefit from the worker's own experience. [K] For example, the delivery drivers are the workers who have direct contact with customers when they take pizzas to their homes. They might be told about which toppings customers would most like to try on the pizzas and the workers could tell Mohamed this. [Ap] If he responded to what customers actually want then he might have a greater chance of reaching his 10% sales increase objective. [A]
>
> If he let workers 'get on with their work' then he might find that because they are being trusted they become more responsible and motivated. Some workers might know the town better than Mohamed and so letting them decide on the best route to take could mean that the pizzas are delivered more quickly and are fresher when the customers come to eat them. [Ap/A]

Your challenge

See whether you can improve this answer. It is well applied to RP but needs a final conclusion/evaluation as the question is asking for the 'most suitable'. A better answer is given online – but write yours out first!

11 Motivation

Learning outcomes

The exercises in this chapter will help you to practise what you have learnt about:

- The importance of motivated workers
- Analysing the ideas of the main motivational theorists
- The different methods of motivating workers
- Evaluating financial methods of motivation
- Evaluating non-financial methods of motivation.

KEY TERMS

Motivation	Performance related pay
Self-actualisation	Profit sharing
Motivating factors (motivators) (Herzberg)	Fringe benefits
Hygiene factors	Job rotation
Job enrichment	Job enlargement
Time-based wage rate	Job redesign
Piece rate	Quality circles
Salary	Worker participation
Commission	Team working
Bonus	

Key skills exercises

Knowledge and understanding

To answer the questions in this chapter, you need to know and understand:

- what motivation means and why motivated employees are important
- ideas of the main motivational theorists (Maslow, Mayo, Taylor, Herzberg, McClelland and Vroom)
- how to differentiate between financial and non-financial methods of motivation
- ways workers can participate in management of a business.

1. Define 'motivation'.
2. State **two** disadvantages that a business might experience from having demotivated employees.
3. State the **five** levels of Maslow's Hierarchy of Needs.
4. State the main findings of Taylor's theory.
5. What were Mayo's main findings?

6   Differentiate between Herzberg's hygiene and motivating factors.
7   What is meant by McClelland's 'achievement motivation'?
8   Explain 'expectancy' as part of Vroom's theory.
9   State **three** methods of financial motivation.
10 State **three** methods of non-financial motivation.
11 State **two** ways in which workers can participate in management of a business.

Knowledge, understanding and application

Remember to use the context provided either by the question or the data response material in your answer.

Shivani's Dresses (SD)

SD was set up 9 years ago. It is now a private limited company. Shivani is the managing director. The company has 47 workers. Most of these are employed making designer dresses and dresses for special occasions such as weddings. These are all expensive and customers have high expectations of both quality and design flair.

Each dress is unique – designed by a small team who work closely together on every customer's order.

The designers are paid a salary. There are three SD managers, including Shivani, who are also paid a salary and have a company pension scheme and health insurance. Dress production workers are paid using a performance related pay (PRP) scheme, which is based on regular target setting and appraisal of each worker's performance.

Shivani has noticed that the dress production workers do not make such an effective team as the dress designers. Some production workers would like more certainty over their pay levels. Despite this, the level of motivation of all SD employees is high. Very few leave each year and customer satisfaction ratings are very high with many repeat orders. Shivani believes that the regular meetings between herself and all employees at which everyone can contribute their views and influence decisions is a major reason for the high motivation level.

12 Explain **two** benefits to SD of a motivated workforce.
13 State **two** forms of non-financial methods of motivation SD is using.
14 Explain **two** possible benefits to SD of using PRP.
15 Outline **two** drawbacks to SD of using this system.

WORKED EXAMPLE

PRP depends on effective target setting and regular appraisal as pay is related to meeting targets. **[K]** It might be difficult to use PRP in this case if one dress is made by several different workers each performing a different task. If one worker is slower than the rest, all workers might fail to meet targets and receive less pay. **[Ap]**

16 State **two** 'fringe benefits' that SD offers its managers.

Knowledge, understanding, application and analysis

The skill of analysis requires that you explain why or how something is an advantage or disadvantage.

17 Analyse **two** reasons why piece rate might be inappropriate for production workers in this case.

18 Analyse **two** benefits that SD might gain from using job enrichment.

19 Analyse, using at least one motivational theorist, the advantages and disadvantages of PRP in this case.

Knowledge, understanding, application, analysis and evaluation

The skill of evaluation requires that you make supported decisions, draw conclusions and give recommendations.

20 Discuss the usefulness of the views of Vroom and Mclelland to Shivani when attempting to motivate SD's workers.

> **TIP**
> For Q20, think about whether one theorist's ideas are more useful in this case – this would be a form of evaluation.

21 Evaluate whether SD should replace the existing pay system with a salary-based payment system for all employees.

Exam-style questions

Paper 1

Section A

1 Explain the term 'self-actualisation'. **[3]**

2 How might a retail business use any **two** methods of financial motivation? **[5]**

Section B

3 a Analyse Taylor's views on employee motivation. **[8]**

   b Discuss whether financial or non-financial methods of employee motivation are likely to be more effective for motivating teachers in a school. **[12]**

Paper 2

Dan's Kitchen (DK)

Dan set up his own café, 'Dan's Kitchen', over 20 years ago. The business now has ten branches. Each branch has a manager and six employees. Three workers prepare meals in the kitchens of each café. They have no qualifications in cooking but Dave gave them a one-day course on how to prepare the most popular dishes. The other three workers serve the meals, make coffee for customers and clear the tables. Dave takes most of the profit out of the business as dividends to himself. Managers are paid a monthly salary. All other employees are paid the legal minimum hourly wage rate.

Dave is concerned about employee motivation. He has to recruit many new workers each year to replace those who leave. Customer complaints about food and service reached a record high last month. The main complaint seems to be that the café workers do not work well together – often arguing in front of customers about whose job it is to sweep the floor, for example.

Last week Dave held a meeting of all café managers to talk about the problems. One proposed a commission payment system for all café workers which would encourage them to work more effectively. She presented the data in Table 11.1 to show how this could operate instead of the hourly rate used at present.

Another manager said at the meeting, 'At my last employer, we had a profit sharing scheme. We were also encouraged to allow participation from the workers.' Dave said that he would consider all of these proposals.

	Existing weekly wage per worker	Weekly revenue – commission to be 20% of this divided between six workers
High season week	$240	$10,000
Average week	$240	$7,200
Low season week	$240	$5,000

Table 11.1: Existing system compared to commission pay system

1. **a** Define the term 'profit sharing'. **[2]**

   b Briefly explain the term 'participation'. **[3]**

2. **a** Refer to Table 11.1. Calculate the difference in weekly wage per worker paid by the two systems during a 'high season week'. **[3]**

   b Comment on your result. **[3]**

3. Analyse the benefits to DK of using non-financial methods of motivation. **[8]**

4. Discuss whether the work of any **two** motivational theorists might help Dan when trying to improve employee motivation. **[11]**

Improve this answer

This is a student's answer to Q4. Skills are shown in brackets to help you.

Two motivational theorists whose ideas that Dan might find useful are Taylor and Herzberg. Taylor believed in 'economic man'. [K] This means that he believed that workers only work for money and they will work harder if more money can be earned. [A] If Dan was to offer higher wages, then café employees would work harder and they would not leave the business so often. [Ap] Piece work would be the best pay system to adopt, according to Taylor. Workers should be paid for each unit they produce and then they will increase output. [A] According to Taylor, workers also need to be told what to do and do not like thinking for themselves. [K]

Herzberg's two-factor theory is quite different. He believed that there were two types of factors that could influence work effort. Firstly, hygiene factors remove dissatisfaction but they do not actively motivate employees. [K] So pay and working conditions, for example, have to be good enough to remove dissatisfaction but after that point then the motivator factors need to be introduced. [A] These are things like 'complete units of work', responsibility, feedback from managers and so on. Once these factors have been put in place, then employees will be much more motivated to work harder as they have been shown more responsibility and trust. [A] So, these are the theories that Dan should refer to.

Your challenge

See whether you can improve this answer. It seems to lack application in the second paragraph and there is no overall evaluation of judgement. The answer needs a good 'concluding' paragraph. A better answer is given online – but write yours out first!

12 Human resource management

Learning outcomes

The exercises in this chapter will help you to practise what you have learnt about:

- The role and purpose of human resource management (HRM)
- Different methods of employee recruitment and selection
- The content and importance of employment contracts
- Different types of employee training
- The importance of employee morale and welfare and how managers can improve them.

KEY TERMS

Human resource management (HRM)
Recruitment
Selection (of employees)
Job description
Person specification
Employment contract
Labour turnover
Training
Induction training

On-the-job training
Off-the-job training
Employee appraisal
Dismissal
Unfair dismissal
Redundancy
Work-life balance
Equality policy
Diversity policy

Key skills exercises

Knowledge and understanding

To answer the questions in this chapter, you need to know and understand:

- **the role of the human resources department including recruitment, selection and training of employees**
- **the formula for the rate of labour turnover**
- **employee training methods**
- **employment contracts**
- **employee welfare and morale.**

1. List **four** responsibilities of a human resources manager.
2. Differentiate between recruitment and selection.
3. Define 'internal recruitment'.
4. State **two** benefits of 'external recruitment'.
5. Differentiate between a job description and a person specification.
6. What is meant by an 'employment contract'?
7. State the formula for labour turnover.
8. Differentiate between 'on-the-job' and 'off-the-job' training.

9 What type of training is usually offered to new employees?
10 Differentiate between 'redundancy' and 'dismissal'.
11 What is meant by the term 'work-life balance'?
12 What would be the aim of a typical 'equality policy'?

Knowledge, understanding and application

Remember to use the context provided either by the question or the data response material in your answer.

City College (CC)

CC is a private school offering IGCSE and A Level qualifications. Asif is the owner of the school and also the Principal. The school employs 46 teachers in 8 subject departments. There are 18 support workers – cleaners, caretakers and technicians. All teaching employees have a written contract but Asif prefers to employ the support workers on an informal basis with no written contract. One support worker complained about this lack of an employment contract. She was so angry that she threatened to 'damage Asif's car' if he did not give her a written contract. She apologised the next day but Asif asked her to leave the school and she lost her job.

Asif spends a lot of time recruiting and selecting new teachers. Table 12.1 shows why. He likes to appoint young teachers as he offers them a low salary and they usually know the most up-to-date teaching methods. Asif has no time to train new recruits so they have to pick up important information and details of the school's procedures listening to and learning from other teachers.

	2016	2017
Teachers employed by CC	44	46
Numbers leaving CC	12	19

Table 12.1: Teaching staff data for CC

Asif has recently appointed two new Heads of Department. The Head of Business has been teaching at CC for several years. He is not aware of the latest teaching methods but is reliable. He is also Asif's golf partner. The Head of Science has just left his job at Capital School to join CC as it is closer to his home. Asif prefers to appoint male heads of department as 'they do not leave to have babies' as Asif once told a School Inspector. Many teachers complained to the Inspector that they had no time to 'themselves' during term time as Asif insisted on attendance at the college even if they had no lessons.

13 Calculate the labour turnover for teaching staff in 2016.

> **WORKED EXAMPLE**
>
> Labour turnover % = $\dfrac{\text{Teachers leaving}}{\text{Number of teachers employed}} \times 100$
>
> $= \dfrac{12}{44} \times 100$
>
> $= 27.3\%$

14 Calculate the labour turnover for teaching staff in 2017.

15 Comment briefly on both these labour turnover results.

16 Was the support worker who lost her job dismissed or made redundant? Briefly explain your answer.

17 Outline **two** benefits to teachers of having employment contracts.

18 Outline **two** disadvantages of inadequate employee induction training at CC.

19 Which methods of recruitment were used for the two Heads of Department. Briefly explain your answer.

Knowledge, understanding, application and analysis

The skill of analysis requires that you explain why or how something could be achieved or why or how something is an advantage or disadvantage.

20 Analyse **two** ways in which employee training could be improved at CC.

21 Analyse how CC could attempt to help employees achieve an effective 'work-life' balance.

22 Analyse **two** advantages to CC of adopting an employee equality policy.

23 Analyse **two** disadvantages to CC of the trend in labour turnover.

> **WORKED EXAMPLE**
>
> A high labour turnover results in high recruitment and selection costs. **[K]** This means that CC will have to spend more on this important HR function so less finance will be available in other areas of the school such as textbooks for Business students. **[Ap]** This is the opportunity cost resulting from a high labour turnover.

Knowledge, understanding, application, analysis and evaluation

The skill of evaluation requires that you make supported decisions, draw conclusions and give recommendations.

24 Recommend whether CC should use internal or external recruitment for Heads of Departments in future.

> **TIP**
> Consider the benefits and drawbacks of both options, for example, the experience of the internal candidates, and provide a justified evaluation.

25 Discuss whether CC should be worried about the trend in labour turnover.

12 Human resource management

Exam-style questions

Paper 1

Section A

1. Explain what is meant by 'induction training'. **[3]**
2. Explain the benefits of internal recruitment for a large retailing business. **[5]**

Section B

3. **a** Analyse how employee training can improve employee effectiveness. **[8]**
   b Discuss the importance of effective recruitment and selection policies for reducing labour turnover in a hotel. **[12]**

Paper 2

> **Transworld Media (TM)**
>
> TM is a news reporting business that provides televised news stories from around the world to television broadcast companies. TM employs 50 journalists and 25 TV camera operators. They can be asked to travel to any country in the world at short notice. TM's reports are used by over 50 national TV broadcasting companies. Some locations are quite dangerous to work in. All TM employees have to be aware of different cultures and traditions in the countries they report from.
>
> Several journalist and camera operator vacancies exist at TM. The HR department has a job description and posted this on the TM website. The job vacancy advert makes it clear that TM's Diversity Policy is a very important part of its human resource management. All employees are given a detailed employment contract. Due to growing demand for experienced journalists and camera operators, TM has occasionally offered jobs to people who have lacked experience. An extensive training programme is then prepared for these new recruits.

1. **a** Define the term 'job description'. **[2]**
   b Briefly explain the term 'human resource management'. **[3]**
2. Outline **two** benefits to TM and its employees of having employment contracts. **[8]**
3. Analyse **two** reasons why TM operates a 'diversity policy'. **[6]**
4. Discuss which methods of training are likely to be most effective at TM. **[11]**

Improve this answer

This is a student's answer to Q3. Skills are shown in brackets to help you.

A diversity policy means that TM has practices and processes in place to make sure that its employees are very mixed in terms of race, gender, religion and age. [K]

One reason for TM wanting to have a diversity policy is to make its news reports more acceptable to its customers – national TV broadcasting companies. [Ap] If all TM reporters were the same gender, age, colour and race then the news reports would not be accepted as being truly representative or unbiased and would be unacceptable to TV viewers in most countries. [A]

Your challenge

See whether you can improve on this answer. There are not enough skills shown to answer the set question. Can you identify why? A better answer is given online – but write yours out first!

13 Further human resource management (A Level only)

Learning outcomes

The exercises in this chapter will help you to practise what you have learnt about:

- Approaches to human resource management (HRM) ('hard' or 'soft' HRM) and flexible working
- Assessing the causes and consequences of poor employee performance
- Evaluating ways to measure and improve employee performance
- The reasons for labour legislation and its likely business consequences
- The benefits of cooperation between employees and employers and Management by Objectives
- The importance of workforce planning
- The role of trade unions.

KEY TERMS

Hard HRM	Workforce planning
Soft HRM	Workforce audit
Part-time employment contract	Trade union
Full-time employment contract	Trade union recognition
Flexi-time contract	Collective bargaining
Outsourcing	Terms of employment
Teleworking	Single-union agreement
Zero-hours contract	No-strike agreement
Labour productivity	Industrial action
Absenteeism	Management by Objectives

Key skills exercises

Knowledge and understanding

To answer the questions in this chapter, you need to know and understand:

- different approaches to employment contracts, labour flexibility and the role of workforce planning
- productivity, absenteeism and employer/employee relations
- workforce planning and factors that influence the workforce plan of a business
- role of the trade unions.

1. Differentiate between a 'hard HRM' approach and a 'soft HRM' approach to managing employees.
2. Differentiate between 'full-time' and 'part-time' employment contracts.
3. What is meant by a 'flexitime' contract?
4. Explain 'teleworking'.
5. Define 'zero-hours' contract.

13 Further human resource management (A Level only)

6 Differentiate between 'core' and 'peripheral' workers.
7 How is labour productivity measured?
8 How is absenteeism measured?
9 State **two** reasons why the state (government) often passes laws that impact on employer/employee relations.
10 Define 'trade union'.
11 What is meant by the term 'collective bargaining'?
12 Define 'single union agreement'.
13 Give **two** examples of 'industrial action' that a workforce can take.
14 State **two** possible benefits of Management by Objectives.

Knowledge, understanding and application

Remember to use the context provided either by the question or the data response material in your answer.

Farah's Fruits (FF)

FF owns several large fruit farms. The fruit is all harvested by hand and up to 70 people are employed to do this. This number falls substantially once all the fruit has been harvested but there is still work to do looking after the fruit trees and bushes for five full time workers. All other employees working on the fruit farms have flexitime contracts with a zero-hours clause. This means that, even during harvest time, employees will only be called in to work and be paid if there is sufficient extra work to do.

Some recent human resources data is given in Table 13.1.

	2016 harvest	2017 harvest
Average workers employed per day	60	64
Total weight of fruit picked [kilos] per year	150,000	145,000
Average number of workers absent each day	6	4

Table 13.1 FF Employment, absenteeism and output data (fruit pickers)

FF also operates a fruit juicing and packing factory. This operates all year because when FF's fruit is not available, additional supplies are imported. Thirty people work in this factory – 28 production workers and 2 supervisors. It is the job of supervisors to train new workers in operating the many different machines used but no off-the-job training is offered.

The factory workers are the only FF employees who are members of a trade union. Three different unions have members within the factory and this can cause problems when FF negotiates pay and conditions with trade union representatives.

The demand for FF fruit juices is increasing by 15% each year. Workers are asking for higher wages because of the extra work involved. Different union representatives are asking for different pay rises for their members. The General Workers Union (GWU) has asked FF's management if they would be interested in agreeing a single union deal so that all FF factory workers had to join this one union.

FF is planning to purchase new machinery to increase labour productivity in both fruit picking and fruit juicing. The human resources manager has to decide how many people to employ after these machines have been bought. In 2016, because of very warm weather, FF had insufficient workers to cope with the huge fruit harvest. Some fruit was not harvested and allowed to rot because of this.

15 Does FF seem to be adopting a 'soft' or a 'hard' approach to HRM? Explain your answer.

16 Outline two factors that FF should consider when planning workforce needs over the next few years.

17 Calculate the labour productivity for 2016 and 2017.

> **WORKED EXAMPLE (FOR 2016)**
>
> $$\text{Labour productivity} = \frac{\text{Output}}{\text{No. of workers}}$$
>
> $$\frac{150{,}000}{60} = 2{,}500 \text{ kilos per year per worker}$$

18 Calculate the rate of absenteeism for 2016 and 2017.

> **WORKED EXAMPLE (FOR 2016)**
>
> $$\text{Absenteeism (\%)} = \left(\frac{\text{No. of workers absent}}{\text{Total workforce}}\right) \times 100$$
>
> $$\left(\frac{6}{60}\right) \times 100 = 10\%$$

19 Outline the possible causes of these changes in employee performance.

Knowledge, understanding, application and analysis

The skill of analysis requires that you explain why or how something is a benefit or a disadvantage.

20 Analyse **two** benefits to FF of flexi-time employment contracts.

21 Analyse **two** possible disadvantages to FF of zero-hours contracts.

> **WORKED EXAMPLE**
>
> Zero-hours contracts mean that there is no security of hours or pay for employees. **[K]** One week they could work 40 hours and the following week no hours at all. Workers will not be loyal to FF if they can get a better employment contract with another business. **[A]** This will mean that during the harvest season FF is short of workers and fruit rots on the trees as not enough workers can be attracted to work for FF with zero-hours contracts. **[Ap/A]**

22 Analyse **two** benefits to FF of conducting a workforce plan.

23 Analyse **two** benefits to FF of agreeing a single union deal with GWU.

13 Further human resource management (A Level only)

Knowledge, understanding, application, analysis and evaluation

The skill of evaluation requires that you make supported decisions, draw conclusions and give recommendations.

24 Recommend whether FF should change its approach to human resource management.

> **TIP**
> Think about whether a different approach should be used for different types of workers. Is it ethical to use the 'hard' approach? Make sure that there is an overall conclusion based on the context of this business.

25 Assess the importance of workforce planning to the future success of FF.

Exam-style questions

Paper 3

Asian Domestic Machines (ADM)

ADM manufactures washing machines, refrigerators and freezers in two factories. Employee performance varies greatly between the factories. Each factory has its own production manager, who have very different views on the best approach to human resource management. In Factory A, flexi-time contracts were introduced three years ago for all new production workers. About 45% of all production workers in this factory now have this form of employment contract. Training is only given to each worker for the specific task to be undertaken. Factory B still offers full-time contracts for 98% of its production workers. Workers are encouraged to become multi-skilled and join quality circles.

ADM managers have recently met to discuss whether they should permit employees to join trade unions. The government has recently passed a law allowing workers to join trade unions if their employers were in agreement. The Chief Executive of ADM thinks that it wastes time to negotiate contracts of employment and annual pay levels with each worker. She also wants to improve communication with employees and encourage workers to become involved in some forms of participation. She thinks that trade union representatives could help to achieve these aims. She has been advised by some of her managers that if the workers all joined the same union, this would give one union's leaders considerable control over ADM.

	Factory A	Factory B
Labour turnover	23%	9%
Number of production workers employed	2,000	3,000
Annual production (units)	300,000	600,000
Number of workers absent on average day	135	150

Table 13.2 HR data for ADM's 2 factories 2017

1 a Refer to Table 13.2. Calculate for both factories:

   i labour productivity [3]

   ii absenteeism. [3]

   b Assess the possible links between measures of employee performance at ADM's factories and the employment contracts offered to employees. [12]

2 Discuss whether ADM should allow trade union membership of its employees. [14]

Improve this answer

This is a student's answer to Q2. Skills are shown in brackets to help you.

Trade Unions are organisations that aim to improve pay and working conditions for their members. [K] TU membership can benefit workers because TU representatives can now bargain or negotiate on their behalf 'collectively'. This means that the TU represents the interest of all members employed within a business and the combined influence of these workers will be greater than if they were not members and tried to bargain individually. [A]

Members can also gain from improved communication from the business. Managers are likely to communicate frequently to TU representatives about the decisions that will affect its members. This information can then be transmitted to the members. This information might not have been given by the business to individual workers without a TU being present. Members can also gain from being represented legally in the event of a dispute between themselves and the employer – for example, about claimed unfair dismissal. [K/A]

Employers can also benefit from their employees belonging to a responsible TU, especially if it is a single TU representing all workers. The business will be able to use the TU as an effective channel of communication. It can now negotiate pay and conditions for all workers with just one (or a few) TU representatives rather than all individual workers and this will save managers time. If there is a single TU, the pay and conditions deal will apply to all members with no danger of another TU trying to get an even better deal for its members. Of course, there might be a greater risk of strike action with TU membership. Strike action is likely to be more effective because workers are TU members as if all members take strike action it will stop business operations completely. However, it is possible for employers to establish a no-strike clause with a single union if some degree of worker/TU participation is allowed. This participation might even be to the advantage of the business if it leads to better decisions and a more committed workforce. [A]

Your challenge

See whether you can improve this answer. Can you identify that it is not at all applied to ADM. This means that the evaluation is weak too as judgements and conclusions must apply clearly to the case study business. A better answer is given online – but write yours out first!

14 Organisational structure (A Level only)

Learning outcomes

The exercises in this chapter will help you to practise what you have learnt about:

- The need for organisational structure
- Analysing and assessing different types of organisational structure and their main features
- Key differences between centralised and decentralised structures
- The conflict between trust and control of employees
- Analysing differences between authority, accountability and responsibility
- Evaluating the appropriateness of different structures to different organisations.

KEY TERMS

Organisational structure	Centralisation
Matrix structure	Decentralisation
Level of hierarchy	Delayering
Chain of command	Line managers
Span of control	Staff managers
Delegation	Informal organisation

Key skills exercises

Knowledge and understanding

To answer the questions in this chapter, you need to know and understand:

- traditional hierarchical organisational structure with its key features (e.g. levels of hierarchy and spans of control)
- alternative organisational structures such as matrix structures
- contrasts between centralisation and decentralisation
- meaning and importance of delegation, responsibility, authority and accountability.

1. What is meant by the term 'hierarchical organisation'?
2. Define 'level of hierarchy'.
3. How does a matrix structure differ from a traditional hierarchical one?
4. What does a 'span of control of five' mean?
5. Define 'chain of command'.
6. Who retains responsibility when authority is delegated?
7. State **two** advantages of a centralised structure.
8. State **two** advantages of a decentralised structure.
9. Differentiate between staff managers and line managers.
10. What is meant by 'informal organisation'?

Knowledge, understanding and application

Remember to use the context provided either by the question or the data response material in your answer.

National Department Stores (NDS)

NDS is a family owned business. The current Managing Director, Chuck, is the fourth generation of the family to control the business. It has 14 stores in country X selling clothing, furniture, electrical appliances and food. Chuck is also planning the creation of an NDS website to allow shoppers to buy online. This will require the employment of more IT specialists. Chuck takes all of the final purchasing decisions made by all of the product departmental heads. Junior managers have little delegated authority. In a recent survey of customers, some complained about the 'outdated' clothing and fashion designs. All shop managers and workers are only allocated to one department (e.g. electrical appliances). There is little contact between employees in one product department and the others. One employee said, 'I am a member of the electricals department but I do not feel a part of the shop itself or of the business.'

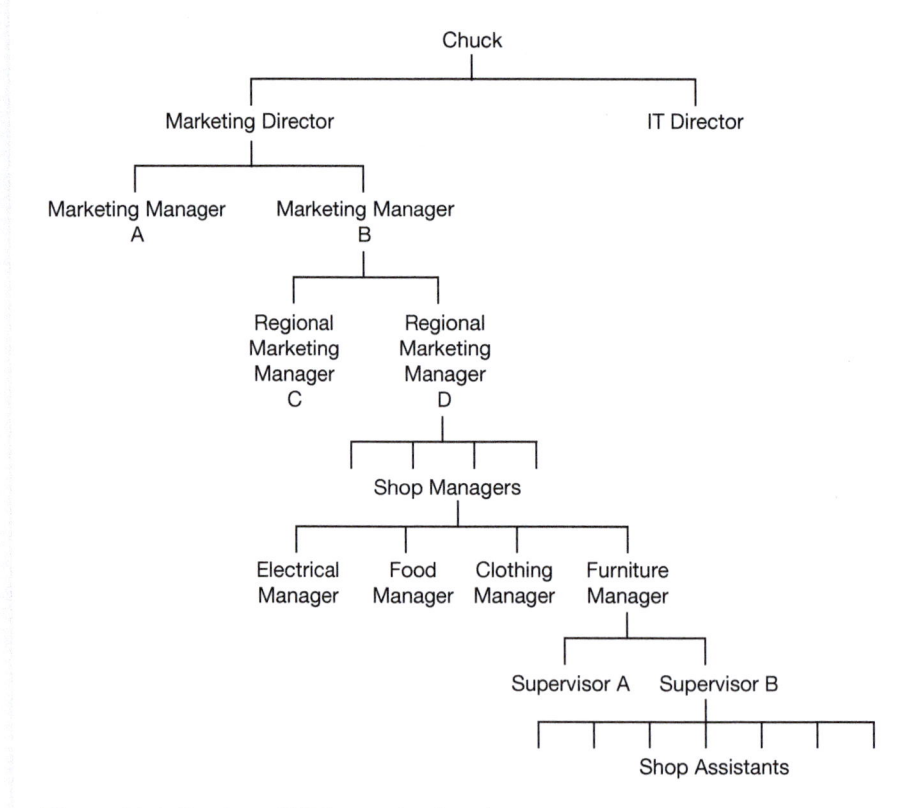

Figure 14.1 Section of NDS organisation chart

11 What is the:

   a Span of control for manager B

   b Span of control for manager D?

12 How many levels of hierarchy are there in the Marketing department?

13 To whom is manager C directly accountable?

14 Identify **one** line manager and **one** staff manager.

15 Explain why the structure shown could not be described as a 'matrix structure'.

14 Organisational structure (A Level only)

> **WORKED EXAMPLE**
>
> NDS is structured as a hierarchy along departmental lines and each manager only ever seems to have experience of one department. **[K/Ap]** Matrix structures would bring teams together drawn from different departments. **[K]**

16 Outline the likely impact on the NDS Marketing department if at least one layer of managers was removed.

Knowledge, understanding, application and analysis

The skill of analysis requires that you explain why or how something is a benefit or a drawback or why or how different elements may affect or impact on each other.

17 Analyse **two** benefits to NDS of changing the organisation to a matrix structure.

> **WORKED EXAMPLE**
>
> A matrix structure creates a 'team-based' organisation. Each team will have representatives from each major functional department and this will improve communication and coordination between departments. **[A]** In the case of NDS, each shop could be treated as a 'team' with representatives from each department within each shop and employees will not feel as if they 'are not part of the shop itself'. **[Ap]**

18 Analyse **two** likely impacts on junior managers in the Marketing department of increased delegation.

19 Analyse **two** possible drawbacks to NDS of rapidly increasing the level of delegation to junior managers.

Knowledge, understanding, application, analysis and evaluation

The skill of evaluation requires that you make supported decisions, draw conclusions and give recommendations.

20 Recommend how NDS should change the structure of the organisation. Justify your answer.

> **TIP**
>
> Think about product-based departments not management functions, matrix organisation, delayering and any other changes you can propose. Provide a clear final recommendation suitable for NDS.

21 Evaluate the impact on the business of becoming a less centralised organisation.

Exam-style questions

Paper 3

World Shoes (WS)

WS is one of Africa's largest shoe manufacturers. It has three factories in different African countries. It sells most of its output through its own shops. It has 213 of these in 20 different countries – most in Africa but some in Southern Europe.

A simplified section of WS's organisational structure is shown in Figure 14.2.

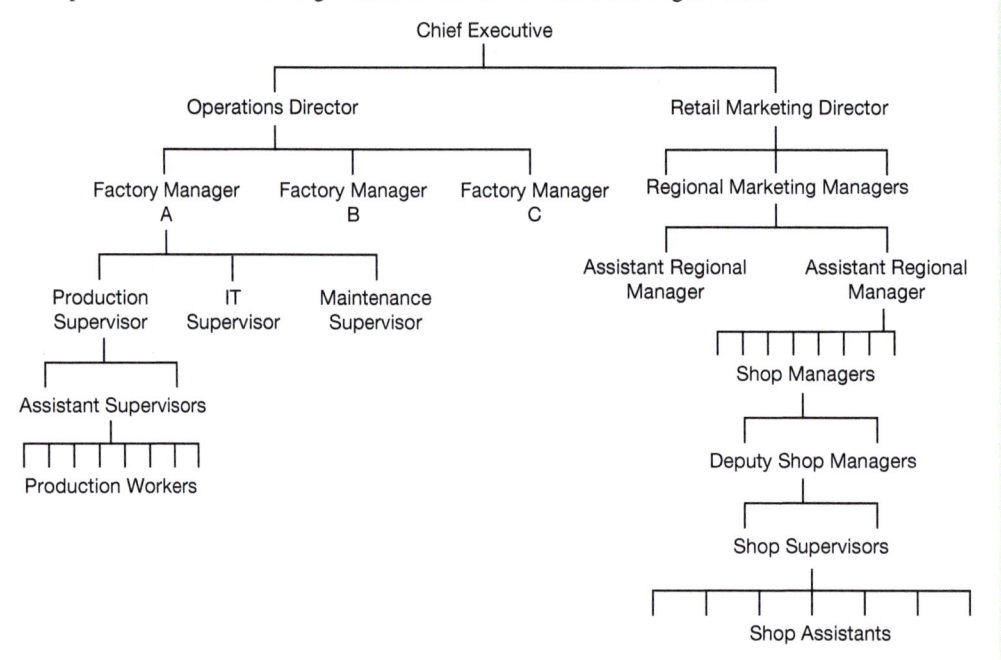

Figure 14.2 WS's organisation chart

A new Chief Executive, Josie, has just been appointed. She is not impressed by the current organisational structure or the centralised approach to decision-making that WS uses. The Board of Directors takes all strategic decisions. Important tactical decisions in each department are taken by the functional directors. Very little decision-making is delegated to lower levels of the organisation or the factory managers or shop managers.

Josie recognises the possible advantages of this centralised approach. She said to the directors at her first Board meeting, 'It means we have the same company policies in operations, human resources and marketing in all of the countries we operate in. This provides consistency and coordination and avoids conflicts. We are able to buy all of our supplies centrally. However, is this approach really suitable for a multinational business which is aiming to expand even further?'

1 Analyse the advantages and disadvantages to WS of having a centralised approach to decision-making. **[10]**

2 Recommend a revised organisational structure for WS that will 'allow for greater delegation and flexibility in future'. Justify your recommendation. **[14]**

14 Organisational structure (A Level only)

Improve this answer

This is a student's answer to Q1. Skills are shown in brackets to help you.

A centralised structure or organisation means that all of the important decisions are taken by senior managers at 'Head Office'. [K] There is very little delegation to lower levels of management or supervisors. [K] This has several advantages to WS. By centralising the purchase of leather and other materials used in shoes, [Ap] the cost per shoe will be lower. The suppliers will be willing to reduce their prices knowing that they are supplying a large quantity. This is called an economy of scale. This will help to make WS's shoes more competitive. [A]

Secondly, taking decisions at the centre means that all factories and all shops owned by WS will be operated in the same way. The shops will all have the same shoes for sale, the same displays and products will be sold at the same prices. [Ap] This will help to achieve consistency and a clear brand image for the company. Customers in all countries will know 'what to expect' from a WS shop. [A]

In the factories, the same HR policies will be used and there will be no feeling from one group of workers that those in another factory are being better paid or better treated. This will help to build a united and cohesive workforce. If a junior manager from one WS factory was promoted to a senior position in another factory, he/she will know exactly how the new factory operates. No induction training will be needed. [A]

Your challenge

See whether you can improve this answer. It is very 'one-sided' and there are no disadvantages – as the question demanded. Can you do better? A better answer is given online – but write yours out first!

15 Business communication (A Level only)

Learning outcomes

The exercises in this chapter will help you to practise what you have learnt about:

- The key features of effective communication
- Analysing different types of communication media – advantages and disadvantages
- Selecting and evaluating appropriate media
- Barriers to communication and evaluate how to overcome them
- The link between communication and business efficiency.

KEY TERMS

Effective communication
Communication media
Information overload
Communication barriers
Formal communication networks
Informal communication

Key skills exercises

Knowledge and understanding

To answer the questions in this chapter, you need to know and understand:

- what different communication media exist and how different media can impact on the effectiveness of communication
- what the barriers of communication are and how to overcome them.

1. What does 'feedback' mean?
2. Give **two** examples of situations in which effective communication would improve business efficiency and help to achieve the required goal.
3. State **two** methods of oral communication.
4. State **two** methods of written communication.
5. State **two** methods of IT-based or electronic communication between managers in the same organisation.
6. Suggest **three** possible barriers to communication.
7. For each of the barriers identified above, suggest **one** way in which it might be overcome.
8. Differentiate between one-way and two-way communication.
9. What is meant by 'vertical communication'?
10. What is meant by 'informal communication'?

15 Business communication (A Level only)

Knowledge, understanding and application

Remember to use the context provided either by the question or the data response material in your answer. One way to do this is to quote relevant sections from the case study in your answer and then explain their relevance.

National Department Stores (NDS) (see also Chapter 14)

NDS directors recently decided to close ten under-performing shops in country Y and open six new shops in country X. The decision to close the country Y shops was not announced for several weeks as the directors did not want the decision to impact on the share price before the Annual General Meeting. However, an internal email was leaked to the newspapers and shop workers in country Y started to discuss the news story one lunchtime. One worker said, 'Not only are we kept in the dark about this decision but we were never asked why we thought sales were falling in our shops. Customers were telling us that the latest fashion and furniture ranges were just not right for our country during the current recession.'

Two weeks later, the directors sent a letter to all regional managers to inform them of the company's plans. It told them to tell the shop managers in the shops that were being closed about the decision. Shop managers were to be instructed to pin a notice on each staff room door. It told the shop workers about the closure, planned for the end of the month.

11 Identify which media of communication NDS uses most often (for example oral, written, visual, electronic).

12 Suggest **two** barriers to effective communication within NDS.

> **WORKED EXAMPLE**
>
> There seems to be too much reliance on written communication – emails and letters – **[Ap]** and letters in particular preventing quick and effective feedback which is a major barrier to effective communication. **[A]**

13 Which 'communication network' seems to be used within NDS?

14 Identify **one** example of informal communication used within NDS.

15 Is one-way or two-way communication used within NDS? Explain your answer.

Knowledge, understanding, application and analysis

The skill of analysis requires that you explain why or how something could be achieved or why or how something is an advantage or disadvantage.

16 Analyse **two** limitations of using noticeboards as a medium of communication at NDS.

17 Analyse **one** way in which NDS is made less efficient as a result of ineffective communication.

Cambridge AS and A Level Business

> **WORKED EXAMPLE**
>
> One way in which NDS is made less efficient by ineffective communication is lack of feedback which makes the business less well-informed about employees' feelings and level of morale. **[K]** By not being allowed to discuss issues, workers are not shown any trust and have no responsibility given to them. This does not meet with Herzberg's 'Motivators' at all and a demotivated workforce will reduce employee motivation and efficiency. **[A]** Employees could have told managers some reasons why sales were so bad in the under-performing shops as they have contact with customers. **[Ap]**

> **TIP**
> For Q19, think about whether two-way communication might be better and which media could best bring this about in this case. Remember to link the communication methods with business efficiency and give a supported final recommendation.

18 Analyse why two-way communication might improve motivation levels within NDS.

Knowledge, understanding, application, analysis and evaluation

The skill of evaluation requires that you make supported decisions, draw conclusions and give recommendations.

19 Recommend how NDS should change the communication media and methods it uses to improve business efficiency.

20 Evaluate the impact on NDS's efficiency if the existing barriers to communication are not overcome.

Exam-style questions

Paper 3

World Shoes (WS) (see also Chapter 14)

'We have just received a huge delivery of red leather and no blue leather. The suppliers are claiming that this is what I ordered on the telephone. Although I posted an order confirmation they claim they never received it. This is not the first time we have had problems with suppliers like this,' complained the Purchasing Director to the Warehouse Manager.

'I see that Head Office has sent us more of those men's summer shoes that we could not sell last year. I told the shop supervisor they were not right for the market in this country but it's a waste of time telling him anything,' said a WS shop assistant to one of her colleagues.

These are just two of the instances of poor communication that the new WS Chief Executive, Josie, is determined to overcome. 'Our communication methods are out of date and we assume that it should only be one-way. Messages seem to pass through so many people that they take too long to reach the person they were intended for. We need to completely revise the methods and media we use for both internal and external communication,' she reported to a recent Board meeting.

15 Business communication (A Level only)

1. Analyse the causes of ineffective communication within WS. **[10]**
2. Recommend how communication might be improved both within WS and between WS and its suppliers. **[14]**

Improve this answer

This is a student's answer to Q1.

Ineffective communication will result in many problems for WS. Firstly, by not making clear to suppliers what materials are needed, the business ends up with too much leather of one colour and none of the other colour. This will cause problems in the warehouse and in the factories as production of blue leather shoes might have to be stopped and sales lost. If some of the red leather has to be sent back to the supplier, then this could be expensive for WS to arrange.

Also, poor communication within WS can result in bad decisions. If two-way communication had been effective, then the shop assistant's comment that a certain style of shoe would not sell, could have been taken back to the regional marketing managers so that the appropriate styles are sent to the right shops. This would help to increase sales in those shops.

Another problem of poor communication at WS is low motivation. The shop assistant seems discouraged and demotivated by her message being ignored. If people are not taken seriously and if their views are not considered in decision-making, then low levels of motivation can be the result. In Maslow's terms, their esteem needs are not being met.

Your challenge

See whether you can improve this answer. The student appears to have misread the question – unfortunately, this happens quite often. This answer is about the consequences of poor communication – not the causes. That is why no skills have been annotated. Can you produce a more effective answer? A better answer is given online – but write yours out first!

Cambridge AS and A Level Business

Unit 2 Research task – Human resources

IKEA in Malaysia – building a strong team

'A happy, friendly and cohesive workforce naturally translates to better business results and customer experience on the sales floor. Hence, as far as possible, we take care of our co-workers' needs and provide a platform and opportunities for building team collaboration and togetherness which reflects our IKEA culture,' says Lydia Song, Human Resource Director for IKEA Singapore, Malaysia and Thailand.

IKEA uses several programmes to allow employees to interact with each other to better understand each other. This leads to a strong team spirit. The company provides finance – called a welfare budget – to allow the management of each business unit to pay for various activities (both formal and informal) to nurture togetherness. IKEA believe that team spirit is very important in each section of each store to provide customers with the best possible service.

These activities include department and management outings, social activities (such as informal get-togethers, social days and family day outings), learning and employee development activities (training sessions and workshops which include team-building activities) as well as business plan kick-off meetings, which include an interactive task for employees (local and overseas) to get to know each other.

These programmes fall under the general co-worker welfare framework, which is operated by the rewards team in HR. The most recent addition to the regular team-building activities IKEA has is the charity day outing. Helped by the IKEA sustainability team, the activity brings together co-workers across the organisation for a good cause – building furniture for an orphanage, cleaning up coastal areas, planting trees and more. This programme was introduced because the organisation is aware its employees are directly impacted by their local environment.

As these activities are generally appreciated and supported by the management, the challenge does not lie in setting up the event or getting employees to attend the event, but rather in getting everyone together at the same time due to the nature of the retail business environment. In order to allow every employee to have a chance to attend the event, IKEA tries to work around the business operations and at times, splits the outings into two sessions.

As a result of these programmes, employees are happier, operations are more efficient and communication is improved, along with a positive impact on the business such as better sales, happier customers and lower labour turnover. To measure and quantify employees' satisfaction in the organisation, IKEA uses two-way communication such as the annual VOICE survey, which all its employees participate in. On a more informal level, the organisation measures the success of its team-building by the number of smiling faces, the general atmosphere in the office, laughter among the team members and how often employees go for lunch together.

Adapted from humanresourcesonline.net

Write a report about how and why two other companies in your country attempt to motivate employees, build team spirit and improve communication. They do not have to be large multinational businesses such as IKEA.

Unit 3
Marketing

16 What is marketing?

Learning outcomes

The exercises in this chapter will help you to practise what you have learnt about:

- The role of marketing
- The link between marketing objectives and business objectives
- Establishing equilibrium price through simple supply and demand analysis
- Understanding and applying the features of markets and marketing: growth; size; share; location; competitors; orientation
- Differentiating between industrial and consumer markets
- Different approaches to marketing: mass marketing and niche marketing
- Understanding the purpose of market segmentation, analysing how it might be achieved and evaluating this strategy.

KEY TERMS

Marketing	Market size
Marketing objectives	Market growth
Marketing strategy	Market share
Market (customer) orientation	Direct competitor
Product orientation	USP – unique selling point
Asset-led marketing	Product differentiation
Societal marketing	Niche marketing
Consumer market	Mass marketing
Industrial market	Market segment
Demand	Market segmentation
Supply	Consumer profile
Equilibrium price	

Key skills exercises

Knowledge and understanding

To answer the questions in this chapter, you need to know and understand:

- **essential principles and concepts of marketing**
- **distinctions between market and product orientation and mass and niche marketing**
- **different ways of segmenting markets.**

1. List **three** typical tasks of a marketing manager.
2. Why is marketing not just about 'selling'?
3. Give **two** examples of common marketing objectives.
4. Why should marketing objectives be linked to corporate objectives?
5. What is meant by the term 'market (or customer) orientation'?
6. What is meant by the term 'product orientation'?

7 Draw a demand and supply diagram showing the equilibrium price.
8 How is market size measured?
9 How is market share measured?
10 Differentiate between 'niche marketing' and 'mass marketing'.
11 Why is product differentiation important?
12 State **two** ways in which markets may be segmented.

Knowledge, understanding and application

Remember to use the context provided either by the question or the data response material in your answer. One way to do this is to quote relevant sections from the case study in your answer.

Global Drink Company (GDC)

GDC produces soft drinks (sodas) from several factories around the world. The brand name used by GDC is 'Sodacola'. This is a well-known name that has been used by GDC for many years. 'Sodacola' is the market-leading cola drink in many countries. The brand name is supported by global promotion campaigns using famous celebrities. Although the company produces many different flavours of Sodacola, the basic recipe is the same. GDC has made no attempts to enter the sports drink market or the markets for diet drinks or 'organic health' drinks. A 'junior' version of its Sodacola drink, with less artificial sweetener and sold in attractive cartons not cans, is the only variation on the basic Sodacola formula.

In 2017, GDC's total sales revenue was $30 billion and the total global market for soft drinks was $120 billion. In 2018, the total market is forecast to be $135 billion and GDC hopes to increase its own revenue by 15%.

Sodacola is made using a traditional but secret recipe. When GDC tried to change this two years ago, in order to save on costly ingredients, consumers responded by reducing demand by 35%. This was despite an expensive promotion campaign. GDC reluctantly returned to the old recipe 18 months ago.

13 Identify whether GDC uses product orientation or market orientation.
14 Explain whether GDC sells to a consumer market or an industrial market.
15 Calculate the forecast percentage increase in the size of the global soft drinks market.
16 Calculate GDC's market share for 2017.

> **WORKED EXAMPLE**
>
> Market share % = $\dfrac{\text{Sales of business}}{\text{Total market sales}} \times 100$
>
> $= \dfrac{\$30b}{\$120b} \times 100$
>
> $= 25\%$

17 Calculate GDC's market share for 2018, assuming that the forecasts are correct.
18 How does GDC currently segment the markets it operates in?
19 Does GDC attempt to differentiate its products? Briefly explain your answer.

Cambridge AS and A Level Business

Knowledge, understanding, application and analysis

The skill of analysis requires that you explain why or how something is a benefit or drawback or why or how different elements may affect or impact on each other.

20 Analyse **two** drawbacks to GDC from using mass marketing.

21 Analyse **two** benefits to GDC from using a market-oriented approach to marketing.

22 Analyse **two** benefits to GDC of 'Sodacola' being market leader with the highest market share.

> **WORKED EXAMPLE**
>
> Market leader means having the highest market share of a particular product market. **[K]** Sodacola is the market leader in many countries it operates in as it has a well-known brand name. **[Ap]** GDC will benefit from supermarkets and other retailers wanting to make sure they hold inventories of this popular drink and they might place it in the most visible and prestigious places in their stores for customers to see it easily. **[A]**

23 Analyse **two** ways that GDC could further segment the markets it operates in.

24 Analyse **two** benefits to GDC of the marketing department coordinating closely with the operations department.

Knowledge, understanding, application, analysis and evaluation

The skill of evaluation requires that you make supported decisions, draw conclusions and give recommendations.

25 Discuss whether further segmentation will increase GDC sales.

> **TIP**
>
> For Q25, consider two or three ways in which GDC could segment its market and the possible costs and benefits of segmenting in these ways. Give an overall conclusion (e.g. the 'best' way to further segment the market).

26 Discuss whether GDC should adopt a market-(customer-)oriented approach to its marketing.

16 What is marketing?

Exam-style questions

Paper 1

Section A

1. What is meant by the term 'mass marketing'? **[3]**
2. Differentiate between consumer markets and industrial markets. **[3]**

Section B

3. **a** Explain, with examples, the difference between market-(customer-)orientation and product orientation. **[8]**

   b Discuss whether niche marketing would allow a car manufacturer of mass-produced family cars to become more profitable. **[12]**

Paper 2

Cathy's Cakes (CC)

CC used to make cakes for sale in the local weekly market. It has expanded greatly to become one of the country's largest cake manufacturing businesses. CC is well known for producing a limited range of popular cakes in such large quantities that costs and therefore retail prices are very low. All CC cakes are sold to large supermarket companies. CC does not make expensive decorated cakes, wedding cakes, birthday cakes or cakes for special festival events.

Cathy is still the managing director. For several years, her marketing objective has been to have the largest market share of any cake producer in the country. There has been considerable market growth in recent years as consumers' incomes have increased. CC's limited range of cakes for the mass market has led to CC's sales not rising at the same rate as the market. Table 16.1 shows recent sales data and a forecast for 2018.

	2017	2018 (forecast)
CC's sales	$3.2m	$3.3m
National cake sales	$14m	$16.8m
CC's market share	See Q2a	19.6%

Table 16.1 Sales data for CC and the national cake market

CC buys in all of the ingredients needed. Sugar is the most important of these. CC is worried about the recent increase in the market price of sugar. Sugar is grown in many countries and depends on good weather conditions.

1. **a** Define the term 'market growth'. **[2]**

   b Briefly explain the term 'marketing objective'. **[3]**

2. **a** Calculate CC's market share in 2017. **[3]**

   b Using your result and Table 16.1, comment on the trend in CC's market share. **[3]**

3 Analyse **one** supply factor and **one** demand factor that could cause the price of sugar used by CC to increase. **[8]**

4 Discuss whether CC should adopt a market segmentation strategy. **[11]**

Improve this answer

This is a student's answer to Q4. Skills are shown in brackets to help you.

Market segmentation is when a business identifies different groups or segments of consumers and selling different products to these groups. [K] The alternative to market segmentation is trying to sell the same type and design of product to all customers. This might be profitable for a product such as computer printer paper which is difficult to differentiate. The customers who need to buy printer paper probably all need the same type and quality of paper no matter what their gender, income, location and so on. So, the costs of segmenting the market could be greater than any increase in revenue so this would make a loss. [A]

The costs of market segmentation can be high. [K] Market research must be done to gain data to be able to split up customers into different groups. Each group should share the same common characteristics e.g. age, gender, income level, social class and so on. Designing and producing different products for these different groups can also be expensive e.g. producing no-sugar soft drinks for people who are dieting as well as the standard sweetened soft drinks. Different promotion campaigns to appeal to different segments of the market might also be needed and this will add to costs compared to just having one standard type of advert and promotion. [A]

Another disadvantage to market segmentation is that by focusing on small segments of the main market, sales might not be high enough to cover all the costs of operating the business so an overall loss might be made. [A]

However, a car manufacturer could benefit from market segmentation and sales and profits might increase. By selling different products to different types of consumers, sales could increase. Not everyone wants the same 'standard' product and consumers might buy a product from another business if they consider that their particular needs and tastes are not being satisfied. As consumer incomes increase with economic growth, consumers want to be seen with branded products that are differentiated and 'aimed' directly at them. So the sale of expensive jewel-encrusted mobile phones is very high in some rich countries – but it would be too expensive to sell to all consumers as a 'standard' mass market product. [A]

So market segmentation can be very profitable as long as the costs of segmenting the market into different distinct groups is not greater than the extra sales revenue that can be gained. [E]

Your challenge

See whether you can improve on this answer. The student seems to have not fully applied the question to the business in the question. The product references should have been to cakes, not printer paper, soft drinks or mobile phones. Can you produce a more effective answer? A better answer is given online – but write yours out first!

17 Market research

Learning outcomes

The exercises in this chapter will help you to practise what you have learnt about:

- Understanding the purpose of market research and the difference between primary and secondary research
- Understanding the methods used to gather data
- Assessing sampling methods
- Analysing and interpreting market research results
- The cost-effectiveness of market research.

KEY TERMS

Market research
Primary research
Secondary research
Quantitative research
Qualitative research
Focus groups
Sample

Random sampling
Systemic sampling
Stratified sampling
Quota sampling
Cluster sampling
Open questions
Closed questions

Arithmetic mean
Mode
Median
Range
Inter-quartile range

Key skills exercises

Knowledge and understanding

To answer the questions in this chapter, you need to know and understand:

- benefits to be gained from market research
- key differences between the collection of primary data and secondary data
- main methods of primary data collection
- sampling methods
- how to interpret market research results and ways of analysing.

1 State **two** benefits of undertaking market research for an entrepreneur.
2 State **two** benefits of primary research.
3 State **two** benefits of secondary research.
4 List **three** possible sources of secondary data.
5 Differentiate between quantitative research and qualitative research.
6 What is meant by 'test marketing'?
7 State **two** possible benefits of using focus groups.
8 State **two** ways in which a business could conduct a consumer survey.

9 Define random sampling.

10 Differentiate between stratified sampling and quota sampling.

11 Outline **two** ways in which the internet can be used to aid market research.

12 Differentiate between the mean and mode of a set of data.

Knowledge, understanding and application

Remember to use the context provided either by the question or the data response material in your answer. One way to do this is to quote relevant sections from the case study in your answer.

Global Drink Company (GDC) (see also Chapter 16)

GDC's Marketing Director now wants the company to produce a wider range of products aimed at the 'youth market' to respond to growing competition. She has asked Asif, a marketing manager employed at Head Office, to be responsible for this. Asif starts by using secondary research he had accessed from the internet. He wanted to find out the age distribution of the country where GDC's Head Office was based. He also purchased a detailed market research report published last year. In addition, he planned detailed primary research. To test out a questionnaire he had drawn up, he selected 50 young GDC employees. One of the questions he asked was: 'How many cans of soft drink do you buy each week?' The results are shown in Table 17.1.

Number of people	Number of drinks bought each week
3	3
5	4
15	5
18	6
6	7
3	8

Table 17.1 First sample of 50: 'How many cans of soft drink do you buy each week'?

After the trial questionnaire, Asif decided to use social media and mobile phones as much as possible to undertake his main primary research. He wanted to find out why young consumers preferred one drink brand over others, what prices they were prepared to pay and what promotion methods they thought were most appealing. He was going to use a sample of 100, split into age groups and then select a certain number from each age range – based on the population data he had researched.

13 Identify which method of sampling Asif is planning to use.

14 Explain two benefits to GDC of using social media for market research.

15 Refer to Table 17.1. What is the modal number of drinks consumed?

16 Calculate the mean number of drinks consumed.

17 Market research

> **WORKED EXAMPLE**
>
> | Number of people (x) | Number of drinks bought each week (f) | fx |
> |---|---|---|
> | 3 | 3 | 9 |
> | 5 | 4 | 20 |
> | 15 | 5 | 75 |
> | 18 | 6 | 108 |
> | 6 | 7 | 42 |
> | 3 | 8 | 24 |
>
> Total fx = 278
>
> Mean = $\frac{278}{50}$ = 5.56 cans per week

17 Outline **two** benefits of the **two** sources of secondary data that Asif used.

18 Outline **two** possible sources of bias in the primary research results.

19 Explain **two** ways in which the market research results could be presented.

Knowledge, understanding, application and analysis

The skill of analysis requires that you explain why or how something is a benefit or drawback.

20 Analyse **two** drawbacks to Asif of the secondary data sources he used.

> **WORKED EXAMPLE**
>
> One drawback of the secondary data is that one of the sources Asif used, a market research report, was out of date. **[K]** It was published last year and the surveys on which it was based might have been done two years ago and out of date data can be inaccurate. **[A]** Consumer tastes can change quickly in the soft drink market so up to date market research data is essential. **[Ap]**

21 Analyse **two** advantages of using a pre-recorded mobile phone questionnaire rather than street interviews.

22 Analyse **one** benefit of any **two** ways of presenting the data to be gathered.

23 Analyse **two** ways in which IT could make Asif's research more cost effective.

Cambridge AS and A Level Business

Knowledge, understanding, application, analysis and evaluation

The skill of evaluation requires that you make supported decisions, draw conclusions and give recommendations.

24 Assess the likely accuracy of the market research data that will be collected by using the methods proposed by the marketing manager.

> **TIP**
> Consider sample size, whether the sample is likely to be truly representative, potential bias, suitability of the questions, suitability of methods. Come to an overall conclusion – could other methods lead to more accurate data?

25 Discuss the most cost-effective ways for GDC to undertake market research.

Exam-style questions

Paper 1

Section A

1 What is meant by the term 'quota sampling'? **[2]**

2 Differentiate between the 'mean' and 'range' of a set of data. **[3]**

Section B

3 a Explain the advantages and disadvantages of using the internet and mobile communications to gather market research data. **[8]**

b Discuss whether a sports clothing manufacturer should mainly use primary research or secondary research to gather market information. **[12]**

Paper 2

> **Get Fit Gym (GFG)**
>
> GFG has been established for 16 years. It was one of the first well-equipped gyms in the area but competitors have opened in recent years. Membership has fallen for each of the last three years. The manager, Suzi, has just finished undertaking some market research. She aimed to find out why membership is falling, what equipment and classes members use most at GFG and what they think of the levels of service being offered. As there are over 2,000 members, she selected a sample of 30. She interviewed them all individually and then formed them into three focus groups. The results of one of the interview questions is shown in Figure 17.1. Suzi is very pleased with the research data that she has collected. She told a meeting of gym employees that using the market research data will 'guarantee the success of GFG in the future'.

17 Market research

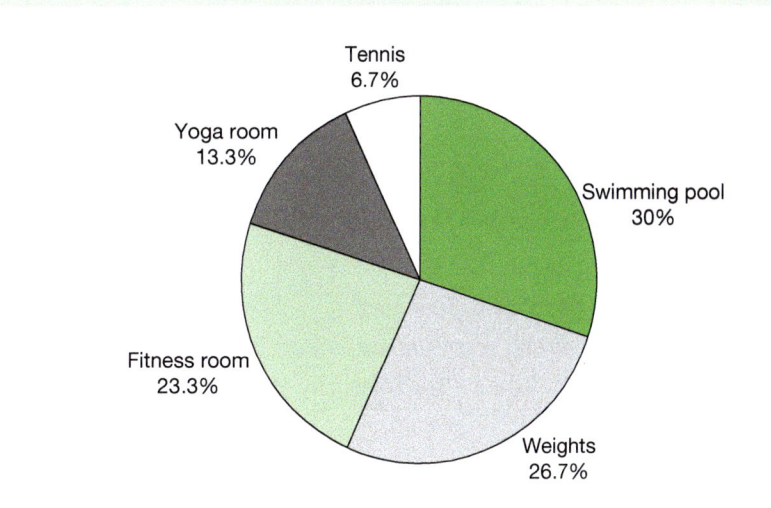

Figure 17.1 Response to the question: 'Which gym facility do you use the most?'

Pie chart values:
- Swimming pool 30%
- Weights 26.7%
- Fitness room 23.3%
- Yoga room 13.3%
- Tennis 6.7%

1 a Define the term 'sample'. **[2]**
  b Briefly explain the term 'focus groups'. **[3]**
2 a Using Figure 17.1, calculate the number of people from the sample of 30 who stated that the swimming pool was the gym facility that they used most. **[3]**
  b Outline the benefit to GFG of using this form of data presentation. **[3]**
3 Analyse the benefits of the primary research methods used by GFG. **[8]**
4 Discuss whether using the market research data will 'guarantee the success of GFG in future'. **[11]**

Improve this answer

This is a student's answer to Q3.

Suzi used a face-to-face interview with each of the sample of 30. She could ask them the questions when they visited the gym and note their answers. They would not have to fill out a questionnaire themselves. [K/Ap]

She then formed them into three focus groups to allow them to discuss qualitative issues that would interest Suzi. These could include 'why some friends have left GFG'; 'what the other gyms offer'; 'how much they charge' and similar issues. [K/Ap] This form of research would gather qualitative information for Suzi. [K]

The sample was small – only 30 out of over 2,000 members – so she could have done this quite quickly. [Ap]

Your challenge

See whether you can improve on this answer – which is not just brief but lacking in important development. In particular, it seems to lack the very important 'skill' of analysis. The points are not developed or clearly explained. A better answer is given online – but write yours out first!

18 The marketing mix – product and price

Learning outcomes

The exercises in this chapter will help you to practise what you have learnt about:

- The components of the marketing mix
- The importance of customer relationship marketing
- Understanding product decisions and analysing the product life cycle
- Understanding, calculating and evaluating price elasticity of demand
- Different pricing strategies/methods
- The importance of pricing to the marketing mix.

KEY TERMS

Marketing mix	Extension strategies
Customer relationship management (CRM)	Price elasticity of demand
Product	Mark-up pricing
Brand	Target pricing
Tangible product attributes	Full-cost pricing
Intangible product attributes	Contribution-cost pricing
Product positioning	Competition-based pricing
Product portfolio analysis	Dynamic pricing
Product life cycle	Penetration pricing
Consumer durable	Market skimming

Key skills exercises

Knowledge and understanding

To answer the questions in this chapter, you need to know and understand:

- **components of the marketing mix, focusing on product and price**
- **product life cycle**
- **different pricing strategies.**

1. State the four elements of the marketing mix.
2. Link each of the 4Ps to the 4Cs.
3. What is the main aim of customer relationship marketing?
4. What is meant by the 'tangible attributes of a product'?
5. Define the term 'brand'.
6. What is meant by 'product positioning'?
7. Draw a simple product life cycle.

8   What is a 'product portfolio'?

9   State the formula for the price elasticity of demand (PED).

10 What does a 'PED of -2' mean?

11 State three determinants of the price of a product.

12 Differentiate between full-cost pricing and contribution-cost pricing.

13 Differentiate between market skimming and penetration pricing (or market penetration pricing).

14 What is meant by 'price discrimination'?

Knowledge, understanding and application

Remember to use the context provided either by the question or the data response material in your answer. One way to do this is to quote relevant sections from the case study in your answer.

Global Drink Company (GDC) (see also Chapters 16 and 17)

Sales of Sodacola branded drinks did not increase at all in the last three months. GDC is preparing to add two new drinks to its product portfolio. As a result of market research, one of the new drinks – 'Top-Pop' – will be aimed at teenagers and the other one – 'SportSoda' – at people who enjoy sport. Both drinks will have features that GDC believe will make them stand out from the competitors. Top-Pop will contain water sourced from mountain streams to appeal to young people's environmental concerns. SportSoda will contain a performance-enhancing blend of minerals and vitamins, developed by GDC's own product development team. Test markets have been used for both products. Sales of these brands changed in the test markets when the prices were reduced, as shown in the following table:

	Top-Pop	SportSoda
Original price	$1	$1.50
Changed price	90 cents	$1.35
Original demand	1,500 cans per week	800 cans per week
Changed demand	1,800 cans per week	840 cans per week

Costly promotion campaigns are planned for both products. Top-Pop in particular is entering a competitive market segment and many teenagers do not have high disposable incomes. A premium high price is being considered for SportSoda but a lower price designed to gain high market share quickly, is planned for Top-Pop.

15 Calculate the PED for Top-Pop based on the test market data

> **WORKED EXAMPLE**
>
> $$PED = \frac{\text{\% change in demand}}{\text{\% change in price}}$$
>
> $$\text{\% change in price} = -10\% = \left(\left[\frac{-10 \text{ cents}}{\$1}\right] \times 100\right)$$
>
> $$\text{\% change in demand} = 20\% = \left(\left[\frac{300}{1,500}\right] \times 100\right)$$
>
> $$PED = \frac{20}{-10} = -2$$

TIP Show all working!

16 Comment on your result.
17 Calculate the PED for SportSoda based on the test market data.
18 Comment on your result.
19 Has GDC attempted to give both new drinks a USP? Explain your answer.
20 At what stage of their product life cycle would you place Sodacola drinks?
21 What are the two pricing methods being considered for the new drinks?
22 Outline two factors that GDC should consider before finally deciding on a price for Top-Pop.

Knowledge, understanding, application and analysis

The skill of analysis requires that you explain why a decision is taken and its likely consequences or how something may affect or impact on other issues.

23 Analyse how GDC could use the PED data in the final pricing decisions.
24 Analyse why GDC might decide to use price discrimination when SportSoda is sold in different countries.
25 Analyse two ways in which GDC could vary the price of Top-Pop as it passes through the stages of its product life cycle.
26 Analyse ways in which the promotion of SportSoda might change as it passes through the stages of its product life cycle.

> **WORKED EXAMPLE**
>
> One way in which the product life cycle will affect promotion decisions for SportSoda is during the introduction phase. **[K]** The product is being sold to the market for the first time so potential customers will need informative adverts about this new product. **[A]** As the soda market has so many brands and is so competitive, the informative advertising will have to be extensive and wide ranging. **[Ap]**

18 The marketing mix – product and price

> **TIP**
> For Q27, consider the way in which the results could be used (e.g. pricing decisions) but also the limitations of the PED calculation and the fact that many other factors can influence sales – not just price.

Knowledge, understanding, application, analysis and evaluation

The skill of evaluation requires that you make supported decisions, draw conclusions and give recommendations.

27 Assess the usefulness of PED to GDC.

28 Discuss whether the pricing decision for either of these products would be very important to its sales success.

Exam-style questions

Paper 1

Section A

1 What is meant by the term 'product portfolio analysis'? **[2]**

2 Differentiate between 'market penetration' and 'market skimming' pricing strategies. **[3]**

Section B

3 **a** Explain how a business can extend the life cycle of one of its existing products. **[8]**

   b Discuss whether a business should use competitive pricing techniques and not cost-based pricing techniques. **[12]**

Paper 2

Voyage Cars (VC)

VC manufactures cars. Currently it sells two models. The Genie is a small car with two doors. It was very popular with young consumers as it is suitable for a 'first' vehicle. However, sales of the Genie have recently started to fall in this increasingly competitive market segment. It is sold at a contribution (or marginal cost) price. It has a small engine and is only available in a limited range of colours. It has been on the market for five years. VC's Marketing Director thinks that the price elasticity of demand for the Genie is quite high.

The Lynx is a fast sports car. It is much more expensive and is targeted at the young career-minded consumer who wants to impress his or her friends. It uses a lot of fuel. It has been on the market for two years and was part of VC's objective to take the company 'up-market'. In three months' time, VC is launching a new model called the EcoStar. It has an electric motor operated from advanced VC-developed batteries. These batteries mean that the EcoStar can travel much further on one 'charge' than other electric cars on the market. Market analysts believe that it will take competitors at least four years before they can launch similarly advanced car models. VC forecasts that the total cost of production of the EcoStar in its first year will be $250 million based on a planned output level of 20,000 cars. VC plans to add a profit mark up of 100% to help pay for the costs of development and the huge promotion campaign planned for its launch.

Cambridge AS and A Level Business

1 a Define 'contribution cost price'. **[2]**

   b Briefly explain the term 'price elasticity of demand'. **[3]**

2 a Calculate the price for EcoStar based on the full-costing method and the company's profit mark-up. **[3]**

   b Outline **one** disadvantage of this pricing method. **[3]**

3 Analyse how marketing decisions for the EcoStar might change when it enters the maturity stage of its life cycle. **[8]**

4 Discuss **two** extension strategies that VC could adopt for the Genie model. **[11]**

Improve this answer

This is a student's answer to Q4. Skills are shown in brackets to help you.

Extension strategies are decisions taken by a business to try to extend the life cycle of a product. [K] They are introduced towards the end of the 'maturity stage' of the life cycle or very early on in the 'decline' stage. The effect of these extension strategies is shown below. [K]

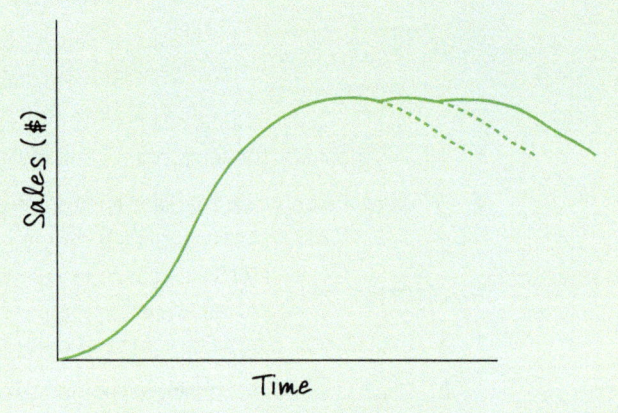

VC could make the Genie available in new exciting colours [K] which would appeal to young consumers, such as students. Just making it available in a limited range of boring colours is certain to be a cause of falling sales, especially as this is a competitive market segment. [Ap/A]

VC could use market research amongst university students to find out what colour cars they really prefer. This information could then be used to decide on the new colours for the Genie. [Ap/A]

VC could also fit a larger engine and adapt the product more to its 'up-market' objective. [K/Ap] This model would then fit in better to the VC product portfolio, especially with the Lynx sports car. The car would appeal to a wider range of potential consumers who wanted more than just a 'cheap to run' car. These two strategies would extend the life of the Genie model and reverse the recent decline in sales. [A]

Your challenge

See whether you can improve on this answer – it seems to lack the very important skill of evaluation.

19 The marketing mix – promotion and place

Learning outcomes

The exercises in this chapter will help you to practise what you have learnt about:

- Sales promotion, advertising, above-the-line and below-the-line promotion
- Promotion campaign objectives
- Factors influencing promotion decisions
- Ways of assessing effectiveness of promotion
- How packaging and branding are important parts of promotion
- Place decisions and distribution channels
- The importance of the internet in marketing
- The importance of a consistent/integrated marketing mix.

KEY TERMS

Promotion	Public relations
Promotion mix	Branding
Above-the-line promotion	Marketing or promotion budget
Advertising	Channel of distribution
Below-the-line promotion	Internet (online) marketing
Sales promotion	E-commerce
Personal selling	Viral marketing
Sponsorship	Integrated (consistent) marketing mix

Key skills exercises

Knowledge and understanding

To answer the questions in this chapter, you need to know and understand:

- **the role of promotion and place as elements of the marketing mix**
- **distinctions between advertising and sales promotion**
- **different sales promotion techniques**
- **the advantages and disadvantages of distribution channels, including the internet.**

1. What is meant by the term 'promotion'?
2. State two possible objectives for a promotion campaign.
3. Differentiate between informative and persuasive advertising.
4. Is 'advertising' an above-the-line form of promotion or is it below-the-line?
5. State three factors that could influence the advertising media used by a business.
6. Define 'sales promotion'.
7. State two examples of sales promotion.

8 What is the main purpose of 'branding'?

9 What is meant by the term 'promotion budget'?

10 Suggest two ways of promoting a product to an industrial market that would not be used for a consumer product.

11 What is meant by a 'one-intermediary channel of distribution'?

12 Define 'e-commerce'.

13 What is meant by the term 'viral marketing'?

14 What is meant by the term 'an integrated marketing mix'?

15 How can packaging support a product's brand image?

Knowledge, understanding and application

Remember to use the context provided either by the question or the data response material in your answer. One way to do this is to quote relevant sections from the case study in your answer.

Voyage Cars (VC) (see also Chapter 18)

VC is now planning the promotion of its new car model, the EcoStar. The directors of the company cannot agree on how big the marketing budget should be. One option is to set it at 5% of the expected first year's revenue gained from EcoStar. A forecast of 20,000 cars has been made and the full cost price of $25,000 agreed. The marketing department plans to spend 60% of this budget on advertising through traditional media.

As the Marketing Director told his colleagues, 'We have to establish the EcoStar brand quickly with a recognisable and differentiated identity and raise customers' expectations if we are to reach the targets set for this product.'

Social media and viral marketing will also be used to promote this product. VC does not sell cars directly to consumers. It sells through garages that act as 'distributors'. They buy cars from VC – either for inventory or as a direct result of a customer order – and handle all of the customer service of displaying and selling the cars. VC does not plan to use all of its existing garage distributors to sell EcoStar as the image and brand of the product is very different from that of the Genie.

16 Suggest **two** possible promotion objectives for VC.

17 Calculate VC's marketing budget if the 'revenue' formula is used.

18 Is VC planning to spend more money on below-the-line promotion or above-the-line promotion? Explain your answer.

19 Explain how successful branding of the EcoStar would help VC.

Knowledge, understanding, application and analysis

The skill of analysis requires that you explain why a business decision is taken or its likely consequences (e.g. advantages and disadvantages).

20 Analyse **two** ways in which VC could make use of the internet in its marketing.

21 Analyse **two** ways in which VC could determine whether its promotion of EcoStar is successful.

19 The marketing mix – promotion and place

> **WORKED EXAMPLE**
>
> One way to analyse the success of this promotion is to survey potential customers. **[K]** They could be asked if they have heard of this new car and whether they thought it had a 'differentiated identity' from other car brands. **[Ap]** If they do think it has a distinct brand, they might be more likely to buy it. **[A]**

22 Analyse **two** advantages to VC of using a one-intermediary channel of distribution.

23 Analyse **two** disadvantages to VC of using a one-intermediary channel of distribution.

Knowledge, understanding, application, analysis and evaluation

The skill of evaluation requires that you make supported decisions, draw conclusions and give recommendations.

24 Recommend the most appropriate methods of promoting EcoStar as it passes through its product life cycle.

25 Recommend an integrated marketing mix for EcoStar.

26 Discuss the importance to EcoStar's success of VC making extensive use of the internet for marketing.

TIP
For Q24, explain why the methods and types of promotion will change over the life cycle of this product. Explain and support your recommendations, to improve the quality of your evaluation.

Exam-style questions

Paper 1

Section A

1 What is meant by the term 'channel of distribution'? **[2]**

2 Differentiate between 'sponsorship' and 'advertising'. **[3]**

Section B

3 **a** Analyse how a perfume manufacturer could use branding to differentiate one of its products. **[8]**

   b Evaluate the importance of promotion to a mobile phone business as a newly developed advanced mobile phone goes through its product life cycle. **[12]**

Paper 2

Magic Cameras (MC)

The market for low-priced cameras has collapsed as mobile phones are now fitted with easy-to-use cameras. However, the market for cameras that offer great flexibility and the potential for 'professional' images with interchangeable lenses is growing. MC has a wide range of medium-priced cameras. It has just finished developing one of the most advanced cameras available to the market, called the ProPix. It is ultra-light, as weight is a common criticism of quality cameras. It is Wi-Fi connectable and is available with a range of excellent lenses for top-quality pictures.

ProPix will take MC into a different market segment. Sales promotion and advertising will be used to attract potential customers' attention. The Marketing Director wants to promote the camera using social media and viral marketing as much as possible. He told other directors, 'We have allocated a marketing budget of $500,000 for ProPix. Only $125,000 of this will be spent on advertising through traditional media as I want to connect with a new type of internet-focused consumers.'

The new camera will be distributed globally using specialist wholesalers and carefully selected retailers. These shops will have to demonstrate to VC that they have employees with a high technical understanding of the ProPix camera.

1. **a** Define 'sales promotion'. **[2]**
   b Briefly explain the term 'viral marketing'. **[3]**
2. **a** What proportion of its ProPix marketing budget does MC plan to spend on advertising? **[3]**
   b Outline **one** way in which the impact of this advertising could be measured. **[3]**
3. Analyse **one** advantage and **one** disadvantage to MC of using a two-intermediary distribution channel. **[8]**
4. Recommend how MC could best use the internet in its marketing for ProPix. Justify your answer. **[11]**

Improve this answer

This is a student's answer to Q3. Skills are shown in brackets to help you.

Using a wholesaler and retailer has big benefits. It means that the manufacturing business does not have the cost of keeping inventories. [K] This frees up capital and space which can be devoted to making the products. [A] Secondly, retailers are specialists in marketing to customers face-to-face. [K] They will spend money on making the shop look attractive and will display the goods attractively. They can answer any questions that customers will have about the cameras and this will give consumers confidence in the product. [A] Manufacturers are not always experienced in selling to consumers and they would have to employ specialist sales staff if they did not use retailers. So using retailers keeps costs lower for manufacturers for two reasons. [A]

Your challenge

See whether you can improve on this answer – it is not only one-sided (did the student misread the question?) but also seems to lack direct application to cameras. A better answer is given online – but write yours out first!

20 Marketing planning (A Level only)

Learning outcomes

The exercises in this chapter will help you to practise what you have learnt about:

- The contents of a marketing plan
- Assessing the usefulness of marketing planning
- Calculating measures of elasticity and evaluate the results
- Analysing the benefits and limitations of new product development
- Evaluating the significance of sales forecasting and assessing the different approaches to sales forecasting
- Assessing the importance of a coordinated marketing mix as part of the marketing plan.

KEY TERMS

Marketing plan
Income elasticity of demand
Promotional elasticity of demand
Cross elasticity of demand
New product development (NPD)
Test marketing
Research and development (R&D)
Sales forecasting

Sales force composite
Delphi method
Jury of experts
Trend
Seasonal fluctuations
Cyclical fluctuations
Random fluctuations

Key skills exercises

Knowledge and understanding

To answer the questions in this chapter, you need to know and understand:

- **the content and purpose of a marketing plan**
- **measures of elasticity (see Chapter 18 for price elasticity of demand)**
- **reasons and evaluation of new product development**
- **methods of sales forecasting.**

1. List **four** of the main elements of a marketing plan.
2. State the formula for income elasticity of demand.
3. What does a promotional elasticity of demand of +2 mean?
4. What does a negative cross elasticity of demand tell us about the relationship between the two products?
5. Define 'research and development (R&D)'.
6. State **two** potential advantages to a business of developing a new product.
7. List **two** reasons why expenditure on R&D might not lead to a successful new product.
8. What is meant by the 'jury of experts' method of sales forecasting?

9 What does the term 'moving average' mean?

10 State **two** possible limitations of the moving average method of sales forecasting.

Knowledge, understanding and application

Remember to use the context provided either by the question or the data response material in your answer. One way to do this is to quote relevant sections from the case study in your answer.

Marta's Ices (MI)

MI is a family-owned ice cream business. It manufactures 45 different flavours of ice cream that are sold through 24 of MI's own shops. The business has expanded in recent years and, on average, now opens two new shops each year. The last four shops the company has opened have not done as well as the sales forecasts predicted. The Marketing Manager of MI believes that the market for standard ice cream may be becoming saturated. There is also evidence that the fall in consumer incomes has had a negative effect. The only ice cream that has increased sales has been the Tropical Fruits Ice, which was promoted heavily during the summer. Sales details are given in Table 20.1

	2016	2017
MI's total ice cream sales (units)	12m	11.4m
Consumer incomes per year (average)	$10,000	$9,800
Sales of Tropical Fruit ice cream (units)	0.5m	0.6m
Promotion budget for Tropical Fruit ice cream	$20,000	$22,000

Table 20.1 Selected sales and other data for MI

The manager thinks that new product development is the best way to increase sales further. Last year MI launched an Ice Cream Cookie, which had such disappointing sales that it was withdrawn after three months. 'We failed to plan for this product and just assumed that the MI reputation would help make it a success,' explained the Marketing Manager. Another new product is now in the development stage. This is called Iced Desserts and is a range of popular desserts that have been mixed with MI ice creams and then frozen. Test market results are encouraging and have led a group of MI senior managers to forecast annual sales at around $1 million in the first year.

MI wants to avoid another sales failure. The marketing department has planned for many months. Last year, the company purchased an external consultant's detailed analysis of the existing ice cream market and MI's place in it. MI's main objective is to achieve 5% of the frozen dessert market in the first year. It will sell the product at a market penetration price during the first three months and then slowly increase price to cover all development and production costs. It will be mainly promoted on road-side posters.

11 Differentiate between MI's current marketing strategy and its marketing tactics.

12 Outline **two** drawbacks to MI of the marketing planning it has undertaken.

13 Calculate the income elasticity of demand for MI's ice cream.

20 Marketing planning (A Level only)

> **WORKED EXAMPLE**
>
> Income elasticity = $\dfrac{\text{\% change in demand}}{\text{\% change in income}}$
>
> % change in demand = $\dfrac{-0.6m}{\$12m} \times 100 = -5\%$
>
> % change in income = $\dfrac{-\$200}{\$10{,}000} \times 100 = -2\%$
>
> Income elasticity of demand for MI ice creams = $\dfrac{-5}{-2} = 2.5$

14 Comment on your result.

15 Calculate the promotional elasticity of demand for Tropical Fruit ice cream, based on the data given.

16 Comment on your result.

17 Outline **two** potential benefits to MI of developing Iced Desserts.

18 Which methods of sales forecasting is MI using? Explain your answer.

Knowledge, understanding, application and analysis

The skill of analysis requires that you explain why or how something is a benefit or limitation.

19 Analyse **two** benefits to MI of marketing planning.

20 Analyse **two** limitations to MI of marketing planning.

21 Analyse **two** benefits of sales forecasting for MI.

22 Analyse **two** benefits to MI of using a coordinated market mix.

Knowledge, understanding, application, analysis and evaluation

The skill of evaluation requires that you make supported decisions, draw conclusions and give recommendations.

23 Assess the importance of marketing planning to the success of Iced Desserts.

> **TIP**
>
> For Q23, try to compare the benefits with the costs/limitations of market planning in this case. Also consider what other factors might influence the success of this new product. Does a marketing plan guarantee the success of a new product?

24 Evaluate the usefulness of sales forecasting to MI.

Exam-style questions

Paper 3

Medical Drugs Incorporated (MDI)

MDI is one of the largest pharmaceutical (medical drug) companies in Europe. It spends around 10% of its annual sales on research and development into new drugs. MDI also manufactures a large range of drugs, including many famous branded drugs for colds, allergies and headaches. MDI's Board of Directors cannot agree on the company's future research and development (R&D) strategy. Some directors want to cut the investment on R&D, close a section of this department and focus resources on expanding production of the branded medicines. The other directors want MDI to stay as a major research company aiming to discover new life-saving drugs. If these drugs can be proven to be safe and effective, then substantial profits can be earned as there will be no close competitors for several years. Data on the R&D spend and recent discoveries of MDI and the other three large drug companies is shown in Table 20.2.

Company	Total R&D investment – 2015–2018 ($m)	Number of new drugs discovered 2015–2018
MDI	$120m	6
A	$300m	12
B	$250m	15
C	$50m	4

Table 20.2 R&D investment and new drugs discovered

Total spending on drugs can vary for several reasons. Government spending cutbacks can reduce the amount that hospitals have available for spending on drugs. The launch of a new drug to relieve allergies can lead to a sharp increase in demand. Seasons can also affect demand. For example, medicines to treat allergies are sold in summer and more drugs that fight the symptoms of colds are sold in winter. MDI wants to forecast sales for its drugs to allow enough resources to be allocated to production and inventory levels. An extract of a time series analysis undertaken by MDI's marketing department is shown in Table 20.3.

Year	Quarter	Sales revenue	8-period moving total	Centred quarterly moving average (trend)	Seasonal variation
2017	3	120	690	90.625	29.375
	4	85	705	x	−8.75
2018	1	80	725	95.625	y
	2	95	750		
	3	125	765		

Table 20.3 Extract of time series analysis undertaken by MDI (All figures $m)

1 a Calculate the values for:

x **[1]**

y **[1]**

b Calculate the forecasted sales for 2019 Q2 if the line of best-fit trend value is 102 and the average seasonal variation for Q2 is −2.3. (All figs in $m). **[1]**

c Discuss the usefulness of sales forecasts based on time series analysis for MDI. **[12]**

2 Evaluate whether MDI should invest further in research and development (R&D). **[14]**

Improve this answer

This is a student's answer to Q1c. Skills are shown in brackets to help you.

Sales forecasts such as the moving average method can be useful. They tell a business what sales will be in the future and this makes planning much easier. [K] By knowing what sales will be, MDI will be able to make sure that the factory is large enough to cope with increased demand for medicines. [A] It can employ more workers if the sales forecasts show that demand is increasing. [K] So without sales forecasts such as the moving average method, MDI will not know how many medicines to make and keep in inventory so customers might be disappointed if not enough products are available. [A]

Your challenge

See whether you can improve on this answer – it is really quite poor. It refers to 'medicines' but the points made could apply to any product. So the answer is not directly applied to the business or product in the case study. It is also rather brief and it is not evaluative. A better answer is given online – but write yours out first!

marketing (A Level only)

Learning outcomes

The exercises in this chapter will help you to practise what you have learnt about:

- Understanding the meaning and causes of globalisation
- The implications for marketing of increased globalisation
- The importance of international marketing
- Assessing and choosing different strategies for international marketing
- Evaluating factors influencing the method of entry into international markets.

KEY TERMS

Globalisation	International marketing
Multinational companies	BRICS
Free international trade	Pan-global marketing
Tariff	Global localisation
Quota	

Key skills exercises

Knowledge and understanding

To answer the questions in this chapter, you need to know and understand:
- **meaning of globalisation and its causes**
- **international marketing opportunities created by globalisation**
- **strategies used by businesses to market products nationally.**

1. What is meant by the term 'globalisation'?
2. List **three** features of globalisation.
3. How has free trade increased globalisation?
4. List **three** reasons why a business might start to sell its products in other countries (international marketing).
5. List **four** ways in which international marketing is different to national marketing.
6. List **four** ways in which a business could enter a foreign market for the first time.
7. Differentiate between 'pan-global marketing' and 'global localisation' marketing.
8. List **three** ways in which a business producing frozen food might have to change the marketing mix of its products if it started to sell them internationally.

20 Marketing planning (A Level only)

Knowledge, understanding and application

Remember to use the context provided either by the question or the data response material in your answer. One way to do this is to quote relevant sections from the case study in your answer.

> ### Value Clothes (VC)
>
> VC is a well-established manufacturer and retailer of 'value clothing' – that is, low priced and of reasonable quality. It operates only in country X, which has quite low average incomes. Unemployment is rising in country X and it has an ageing population. VC's range of clothes is traditionally designed and does not follow the latest fashions. VC has several important competitors and the overall clothing market is not growing.
>
> VC's directors are planning to expand the business by selling clothes in country Y for the first time. This country has average income levels that are increasing rapidly. It has a youthful population that is increasingly attracted to buying products with well-known brand names. VC plans to buy its own shop premises in country Y to distribute its clothes there. VC's Marketing Manager suggested, 'By selling our clothes in country Y at the same low prices we should be able to establish a high market share quickly.'

9 Which method of entering the market of country Y is VC planning to use?

10 Outline **two** benefits to VC of marketing its products internationally.

> ### WORKED EXAMPLE
>
> VC can benefit from the greater sales potential in country Y **[K]** as it has high average income levels. **[Ap]** The market is not growing in country X so to start selling clothes to country Y will give a chance of increased total sales. **[Ap]**

11 Is VC planning to use 'pan-global' or 'global localisation' marketing? Explain your answer.

Knowledge, understanding, application and analysis

The skill of analysis requires that you explain how or why something could happen or the advantages or problems that could result from a decision.

12 Analyse **two** other ways in which VC could enter the market in country Y.

13 Analyse **two** problems that VC could experience in country Y if it made no changes to its marketing mix.

14 Analyse **two** problems for VC if it decides to adopt a 'global localisation' approach to marketing its products in country Y.

Cambridge AS and A Level Business

> **WORKED EXAMPLE**
>
> One problem would be higher costs. **[K]** A global localisation approach will mean undertaking detailed market research to find out the needs and tastes of local consumers to allow appropriate product decisions to be taken. **[A]** VC seems to make traditional clothes and these are unlikely to be popular in country Y with a 'youthful' population. **[Ap]**

Knowledge, understanding, application, analysis and evaluation

The skill of evaluation requires that you make supported decisions, draw conclusions and give recommendations.

15 Assess the factors that will influence the success of VC's first attempt at international marketing.

> **TIP**
>
> For Q15, try to weigh up whether VC's approach to marketing in country Y for the first time is likely to be successful. How should 'success' be measured? By level of sales and/or profits? By market share? Also consider what factors might influence the success of this strategy.

16 Recommend which marketing strategy VC should use when selling its products in country Y.

Exam-style questions

Paper 3

Aisha's Processed Foods (APF)

APF specialises in producing a range of 'ready meals' and frozen food products. These are sold to supermarkets in country P. APF does not own any retail outlets. APF's production costs are low as the business employs many immigrant workers on the minimum wage. The market for ready meals and frozen food is very competitive, especially since the government of country P decided last year that the country should join a large 'free trade area'. Imports of all food products have increased, especially those that meet the needs of the many different ethnic groups that live in country P.

As the processed food market in country P is mature or 'saturated', the directors of APF have decided to market some food products internationally. This expansion will require additional finance and APF has been able to obtain capital from a foreign investor. Banks in country P were reluctant to lend to the company. APF plans to start by selling products to country R, a member of the same free-trade group.

21 Globalisation and international marketing (A Level only)

The directors of APF now have to decide on which marketing strategy to adopt for selling to country R. Details of the two options are given in Table 21.1.

	Marketing strategy A	**Marketing strategy B**
Products	No change in products – this will allow quicker entry into a foreign market than developing new products.	Some new products adapted for new market to reflect local tastes/cultures. Will take time and finance to develop these.
Prices	Same as in country P – full cost price with small profit margin – converted into foreign currency.	Low prices to establish market share. May not cover full cost of the products to start with.
Promotion	Same packaging, sales promotions and advertising as now – but change in language for foreign market.	Expensive new promotions such as advertisements that clearly use local people and make local culture references.
Place/distribution	Try to set up direct links with supermarkets in country R and distribute directly to these shops.	Sell through local distributor to supermarkets in country R – this uses local distribution system but an additional intermediary.

Table 21.1 The two alternative marketing strategies for APF

1 Analyse the impact that globalisation is having on APF. **[10]**
2 Recommend whether APF should adopt marketing strategy A or marketing strategy B. Justify your answer. **[16]**

Improve this answer

This is a student's answer to Q1. Skills are shown in brackets to help you.

Globalisation is when countries agree to trade with no trade barriers and allow the free movement of capital and, increasingly, workers. [K]

Globalisation is both helping APF and acting as a constraint. AFP is experiencing more competition in country P's market. However, it will be able to import food ingredients more cheaply without tariffs. [K/Ap]

APF will be able to sell its own products more cheaply to other members of the free trade area. It can raise capital more easily from other countries as it did in this case when the banks in country P were reluctant to lend to the business. [Ap] APF can employ more migrant workers as a result of globalisation as there is freer movement of workers between many countries. [K]

Your challenge

See whether you can improve on this answer – it is not only quite brief but lacks any detailed analysis. The consequences – positive or negative – of globalisation on APF are not really developed or explained. A better answer is given online – but write yours out first!

Unit 3 Research task – Marketing

The Apple success story

Some business analysts describe Apple Inc. as the most successful business in all of history. It was started in 1976. It has grown to become the most valuable company in the world (by market values of its shares). Its brand name and logo are valued more highly than those of any other business. Total global revenue exceeds $250 billion and this figure is much higher than many countries' Gross Domestic Product. Its new product launches – such as that for iPhone 7 – have become international media events. Customers have been known to queue for days outside Apple stores to even have a chance of purchasing the latest newly released product.

As well as operating 478 physical shops in 17 different countries, it also operates the online Apple store and the iTunes Store which is the world's most successful online music retailer. Apple Inc. uses many different forms of promotion but it is increasingly using online methods and social media to communicate with existing and potential consumers. None of these advertisements or social media sites carry details about Apple Inc.'s 'sale prices' or 'special discounts'. Competing with rivals by reducing prices is just not Apple Inc.'s approach.

How can this incredible success be explained?

Write a report about the reasons for Apple's marketing success story. Focus on its marketing mix and try to assess whether it is just one element of this mix that is the most important factor behind its success. You might conclude, on the other hand, that no single factor is important and that Apple's marketing and sales growth can be explained by it having 'the best coordinated marketing mix in history'!

Unit 4
Operations and project management

22 The nature of operations

Learning outcomes

The exercises in this chapter will help you to practise what you have learnt about:

- The meaning of operations management
- Understanding the production process and how value can be added
- Differentiating between production and productivity; efficiency and effectiveness
- The advantages and limitations of labour-intensive production and capital-intensive production processes.

KEY TERMS

Added value	Efficiency
Intellectual capital	Effectiveness
Production	Labour intensive
Level of production	Capital intensive
Productivity	

Key skills exercises

Knowledge and understanding

To answer the questions in this chapter, you need to know and understand:

- the meaning of operations and operations management
- the transformation process
- important differences between production and productivity and efficiency and effectiveness
- important differences between labour intensive production and capital intensive production.

1. What is meant by the term 'production'?
2. List **three** inputs needed in the production process.
3. Differentiate between capital (e.g. machinery) and intellectual capital.
4. State **two** ways in which the production process can help a business add value to bought-in inputs.
5. Explain how it is possible for the level of production to increase but for the rate of productivity to fall.
6. State the formula for labour productivity.
7. Outline **two** ways in which a manufacturing business could increase labour productivity.
8. Differentiate between an efficient production process and an effective production process.
9. State **two** examples of industries where labour-intensive production is still common.

10 Outline **two** limitations of labour-intensive production.

11 Outline **two** factors that will influence the decision by a business whether to adopt labour-intensive or capital-intensive production processes.

12 Outline **two** limitations of capital-intensive production processes.

Knowledge, understanding and application

Remember to use the context provided either by the question or the data response material in your answer. One way to do this is to quote relevant sections from the case study in your answer.

Fast Food Kitchen (FFK)

FFK has a problem. The demand for burgers and taco wraps outstrips the output levels being achieved in the kitchen. The business has an excellent reputation for 'home cooked food' but service levels are poor. Customers complain about the long wait for food to be served and some leave before the food they have ordered arrives. This leads to food wastage and profits are falling. FFK employs two excellent chefs and some other kitchen workers. It has recruited three more kitchen employees and they began work at the start of month 3.

Production of the food sold by FFK uses a slow process, with each stage of cutting meat and vegetables, preparing the buns or taco wraps, cooking the ingredients, putting the food on a plate and garnishing it with salad being undertaken by teams of workers. They use simple equipment such as knives, a meat mincer and one gas cooker. Details of production levels and employment levels in the kitchen are shown below:

	Month 1	Month 2	Month 3
Number of meals produced	20,000	21,000	26,000
Number of employees in kitchen	10	11	14
Labour productivity per month	2,000	See Q13	See Q14

Table 22.1 Production levels and numbers employed in kitchen

FFK's managers are planning to purchase an automatic burger-making machine as well as a flow production oven and grill that can be digitally controlled by a single worker.

13 Calculate labour productivity in month 2.

WORKED EXAMPLE

$$\text{Labour productivity per time period} = \frac{\text{Output in time period}}{\text{Number employed}}$$

$$\text{Month 2 labour productivity} = \frac{21,000}{11} = 1909 \text{ meals per month per employee}$$

14 Calculate labour productivity in month 3.

15 Comment on the trend in labour productivity.

Cambridge AS and A Level Business

16 Calculate the percentage increase in production between month 2 and month 3.

17 Does FFK currently use a labour-intensive or capital-intensive production process? Explain your answer.

Knowledge, understanding, application and analysis

The skill of analysis requires that you explain 'why' or 'how' a likely outcome might occur or the consequences of the outcome.

18 Analyse **two** problems for FFK as a result of the trend in labour productivity.

19 Analyse **two** possible reasons why there is this trend in labour productivity.

20 Analyse **two** problems that might result for FFK as a result of introducing a capital-intensive production process.

> ### WORKED EXAMPLE
>
> One problem is that capital equipment is expensive and requires finance. **[K]** The purchase of an 'automatic burger-making machine' will require finance. **[Ap]** This could be a problem for FFK as profit is falling so there might be less cash available in the business for capital equipment. **[Ap/A]** FFK might have to take out a loan to make the business capital intensive and the interest on the loan could reduce profit further. **[A]**

21 Apart from buying new machinery, explain **two** ways that FFK could use to try to increase labour productivity.

22 Analyse how the operations process at FFK helps to add value.

Knowledge, understanding, application, analysis and evaluation

The skill of evaluation requires that you make supported decisions, draw conclusions and give recommendations.

23 Discuss whether FFK should switch to capital intensive production methods.

> ### TIP
> For Q23, try to weigh up whether FFK could lose some of its appeal to customers if meals are not fully 'home cooked' and not prepared by hand. The cost of the equipment is important. Will kitchen workers be made redundant? Will this impact on motivation for those who remain? Will capital-intensive production solve the poor service problem?

22 The nature of operations

Exam-style questions

Paper 1

Section A

1 Briefly explain what is meant by 'intellectual capital'. **[3]**

2 Briefly explain what is meant by 'the production (or transformation) process'. **[3]**

Section B

3 **a** With the use of examples, differentiate between production levels and levels of productivity. **[8]**

   b Discuss whether a manufacturer of hand-built racing bicycles should switch to capital-intensive methods of production to improve labour productivity. **[12]**

Paper 2

Shahzad Carpets and Rugs (SCR)

SCR is well known for the quality of the carpets and rugs it makes. All of its products are handmade using old hand-held tools and techniques developed over many years. Demand is high as the styles and patterns made by SCR are selected after undertaking market research. Consumers often say that SCR carpets are the best-quality products available. There is a waiting list for SCR's largest rugs and carpets despite the recent recruitment of ten new workers.

Labour turnover is high at SCR. Workers complain of long hours and strict management controls. They also do not like untrained workers being allowed to 'learn on the job' and that any mistakes made have to be corrected by the experienced workers. The Operations Manager reported to his colleagues recently that 'Production effectiveness' is high but our level of efficiency is low'. Look at the data in Table 22.2.

	Month 1	Month 2	Month 3
Number of carpets and rugs made	180	183	192
Number of production workers	45	47	55
Labour productivity	4	3.9	

Table 22.2 Operations data for SCR

The Operations Manager wants to increase labour productivity. He wants to start making carpets using computer-controlled machinery. 'These could more than double the rate of labour productivity,' he said. Other managers do not want to use machines and think that there are other ways in which labour productivity could be increased.

1 **a** Define the term 'efficiency'. **[2]**

   b Briefly explain the term 'Production effectiveness'. **[3]**

2 **a** Calculate labour productivity for SCR in month 3. **[3]**

   b Comment on the trend in labour productivity. **[3]**

3   Analyse **two** ways in which labour productivity could be increased, without purchasing new capital equipment. [8]

4   Discuss whether the decision to switch to capital-intensive production is the right one for SCR to take. [11]

Improve this answer

This is a student's answer to question 4. Skills are shown in brackets to help you.

Capital-intensive production means using a lot of machinery to produce a product – and not very many workers. [K] A car assembly line using automatic robots would be a good example of capital-intensive production. This method of production increases output and more importantly it increases labour productivity. [A] Each worker can now produce many more cars or units of output per week with machines than they could have done using labour-intensive production process. [A]

High labour productivity will reduce the labour cost per unit and make SCR much more competitive as well as increasing output. [A] Machines can work all day and a new shift of workers can be called in and this will increase output. This is what the Operations Manager wants. To increase output to reduce the waiting lists so of course SCR should switch to capital-intensive methods of production. [E]

Your challenge

See whether you can improve this answer. It seems to lack an important 'skill' – that of direct application to the case study business. In addition, the conclusion is weak and not supported by the arguments used. A better answer is given online – but write yours out first!

23 Operations planning (AS and A Level)

Learning outcomes

The exercises in this chapter will help you to practise what you have learnt about:

- Understanding operations planning and the influence of marketing, resources and information technology
- Understanding the need for flexibility and process innovation
- Differentiating between production methods (job, batch, flow, mass customisation)
- The factors that influence the choice of production methods used
- Location decisions and the factors that influence them
- Analysing the scale of production
- Enterprise Resource Planning (A Level only).

KEY TERMS

Operations planning	Location – qualitative factors
Computer Aided Design (CAD)	Multi-site location
Computer Aided Manufacturing (CAM)	Offshoring
Operational flexibility	Multinational
Process innovation	Trade barriers
Job production	Scale of operation
Batch production	Economics of scale
Flow production	Diseconomies of scale
Mass customisation	Enterprise Resource Planning (A Level only)
Optimal location	Supply chain (A Level only)
Location – quantitative factors	Sustainability (A Level only)

Key skills exercises

Knowledge and understanding

To answer the questions in this chapter, you need to know and understand:

- the meaning of operations planning and operational flexibility and influence of technology
- the important differences between production methods
- the factors that influence the important operational decision of location
- the impact that the scale of operation can have on business efficiency.

1. What is meant by the term 'job production'?
2. Differentiate between 'batch production' and 'flow production'.
3. Give **one** example of process innovation.
4. State **two** benefits of CAM.
5. State **two** benefits of mass customisation.
6. Give **two** examples of quantitative factors that influence business location decisions.

7 Give **two** examples of qualitative factors that influence business location decisions.
8 State **two** possible reasons why a business might offshore some of its operations.
9 Define 'economies of scale'.
10 Give **two** examples of economies of scale that a business might benefit from as it increases its scale of production.
11 What is meant by the term 'supply chain'?
12 Define 'enterprise resource planning'. (A Level only)

Knowledge, understanding and application

Remember to use the context provided either by the question or the data response material in your answer. One way to do this is to outline why advantages, disadvantages, benefits and limitations apply particularly to the case study business.

Folding Bike Co (FBC)

Dashin started making bicycles in his garage 25 years ago. He had designed a folding bicycle that fits into a small suitcase. Once out of the case, it can be quickly unfolded to become a bicycle suitable for small adults or children. Dashin made the first bicycles by hand. He talked to customers – mainly friends and relatives to start with – about the colour of frame and the type of saddle they wanted. Then he made each one himself using mainly bought-in components but some parts he made himself. Dashin called his business the Folding Bike Co.

Now, 25 years later, FBC has a factory on the edge of the capital city. Production uses a computer-controlled flow line. Some components are still bought in from suppliers. Individual variations in bicycle design and the features demanded by each customer can be incorporated into this production process. The scale of operation of the business has increased in recent years. This has impacted on the unit cost per bicycle – see Table 23.1.

Annual output	10,000	100,000	200,000
Unit bicycle cost of production	$135	$105	$95

Table 23.1 Increased output results in lower unit cost

Some production is also offshored. When FBC is very busy, a supplier in Asia produces bicycle kits, at low cost, that are then quickly assembled by FBC in its factory. This increases total output. Transport hold-ups have caused some supply problems and the quality of some of the kits is poor.

Several different designs and sizes of folding bicycles are now made by FBC. Using computers to simulate the completed designs speeded up this process. Using CAM also makes the company more flexible to meet the changing demands of consumers both in the domestic and foreign markets.

FBC is now considering getting a bank loan to finance relocation to a larger site. Some data about two possible locations are shown in Table 23.2.

	Location A	Location B
Annual fixed-site costs	$6m	$9m
Maximum annual potential output	300,000	500,000
Distance from main city	40 km	10 km
Distance from major sea port	220 km	250 km

Table 23.2 Selected data about two alternative locations for FBC

13 Comment on the trend in unit cost as the business has expanded its scale of operation.
14 Outline **two** possible reasons to explain this trend.
15 Suggest **two** ways in which FBC benefits from using CAM.
16 Which method of production was originally used within FBC?
17 Comment on **two** likely economies of scale that FBC might experience if it continues to expand.
18 Give **two** examples of operational flexibility within FBC.

> **WORKED EXAMPLE**
>
> One example of flexibility is the use by FBC of a computer-controlled production line (CAM). **[K]** This allows the business to introduce 'individual variations in bike design'. **[Ap]**

Knowledge, understanding, application and analysis

The skill of analysis requires that you explain why or how something is a benefit or drawback.

19 Explain **two** benefits to FBC resulting from its use of mass customisation.
20 Analyse **one** benefit to FBC from declining unit costs as its scale of operation increases.
21 Analyse **one** benefit to FBC of CAM.

> **WORKED EXAMPLE**
>
> One benefit is that CAM is making FBC more flexible. **[K]** By showing customers what a new bike design looks like on computer screen or by drawing on the screen the style of bike the consumer is asking for, different models can be introduced more quickly. This makes FBC more competitive compared to bike makers that do not use CAM. **[Ap/A]**

22 Analyse **two** benefits to FBC of operational flexibility.
23 Analyse **two** potential problems that FBC might experience following its decision to offshore some operations.
24 Analyse **two** benefits to FBC of using Enterprise Resource Planning (ERP).

Knowledge, understanding, application, analysis and evaluation

The skill of evaluation requires that you make supported decisions, draw conclusions and give recommendations.

25 Discuss whether FBC should offshore a higher proportion of its total output.

> **TIP**
>
> For Q25, analyse the advantages and potential drawbacks to FBC from offshoring more output – and come to a reasoned conclusion/recommendation.

26 Recommend which location should be chosen for the new factory.

Exam-style questions

Paper 1

Section A

1. Briefly explain the term 'process innovation'. **[3]**
2. Briefly explain the term 'mass customisation'. **[3]**

Section B

3. **a** With the use of examples, analyse the difference between economies of scale and diseconomies of scale. **[8]** See Improve this answer on next page.

   b Discuss the major factors likely to influence the location of a new state-owned hospital. **[12]**

Paper 2

> **Spartacus Sports Shoes (SSS)**
>
> SSS produce exclusive and expensive sports shoes for top athletes. They are also bought by wealthy fashion-conscious consumers who want to be seen in the 'sportiest shoes on the planet' (an SSS advertising claim!).
>
> Each style of shoe is made to a customer's special requests for size, colour, type of material and decorative features. Customers can even help design their own shoes online by use of an interactive tool on the SSS website. This form of CAD helps to give each customer a sense of ownership of their own shoe design.
>
> SSS shoes are made in a small factory on an industrial estate. Several of the other businesses on this estate supply SSS with important materials and services. The company directors relocated the business to the estate four months ago. The site is expensive as it is near the main city and close to a good transport network. SSS has difficulty in recruiting suitably experienced production workers. The Managing Director recently told her colleagues, 'I am not sure we made the right decision to locate here. Do the external economies of scale make up for the higher rental costs?'
>
> SSS has grown considerably in recent years. Table 23.3 shows the rising output and changing unit cost of producing each pair of shoes.
>
> | Annual output | 500 pairs | 2,000 pairs | 10,000 pairs |
> |---|---|---|---|
> | Unit cost per pair of shoes | $250 | $225 | $235 |
>
> **Table 23.3** Rising SSS output in recent years and the unit cost per pair of shoes
>
> SSS has developed a new style of shoe – called the SX3 – to be sold to the mass market. It will use batch production, not job production. Each batch will contain the same design of shoe but there will be batches of different sizes.

1. **a** Define the term 'CAD' (Computer Aided Design). **[2]**

   b Briefly explain the term 'external economies of scale'. **[3]**

2 a Calculate the percentage change in unit cost as output increased from 500 pairs to 2,000 pairs per year. **[3]**

b Comment on the change in unit cost when annual output increased to 10,000 pairs. **[3]**

3 Analyse **two** benefits to SSS of using batch production for the SX3 shoe. **[8]**

4 Discuss whether the decision to relocate to the industrial estate was the right one for the company to take. **[11]**

Paper 3

1 Analyse the benefits to SSS of adopting Enterprise Resource Planning. **[10]**

Improve this answer

This is a student's answer to Paper 1 Q3a. Skills are shown in brackets to help you.

Economies of scale are factors that lead to a fall in average or unit costs of production when a business expands its scale of operation. [K] These cost reductions therefore help to make the business more efficient and competitive. [A]

Diseconomies of scale lead to higher average or unit costs when a business increases its scale of operation. [K] This means that the business becomes less efficient and less competitive. [A]

So some factors can lead to lower average costs and others can lead to higher unit costs.

Your challenge

See whether you can improve this brief answer. It seems to lack a very important 'skill' of application through the use of examples. A better answer is given online – but write yours out first!

24 Inventory management

Learning outcomes

The exercises in this chapter will help you to practise what you have learnt about:

- Understanding the reasons for holding inventories and the costs and benefits of inventories
- The advantages and disadvantages of traditional inventory holding systems
- Evaluating the just-in-time (JIT) inventory management system.

KEY TERMS

Inventory
Economic order quantity
Buffer inventories

Re-order quantity
Lead time
Just-in-time (JIT)

Key skills exercises

Knowledge and understanding

To answer the questions in this chapter, you need to know and understand:

- **the importance of inventory holding and inventory management**
- **the costs and benefits of holding inventories**
- **the risks and benefits of JIT.**

1. What is meant by the term 'inventory'?
2. State **three** costs of holding inventories.
3. What costs are linked to running out of inventories?
4. State **three** types of inventory.
5. What is meant by 'buffer inventory'?
6. Why is a long lead time a problem when re-ordering inventory?
7. What is meant by 'just-in-time'?
8. State **three** conditions for JIT inventory control to be effective.

24 Inventory management

Knowledge, understanding and application

Remember to use the context provided either by the question or the data response material in your answer. One way to do this is to outline why advantages, disadvantages, benefits and limitations apply particularly to the case study business.

Folding Bike Co (FBC) (see also Chapter 23)

FBC holds a high level of inventories of most components that it buys in – especially imported ones. The inventory control chart for one type of bicycle tyre is shown in Figure 24.1.

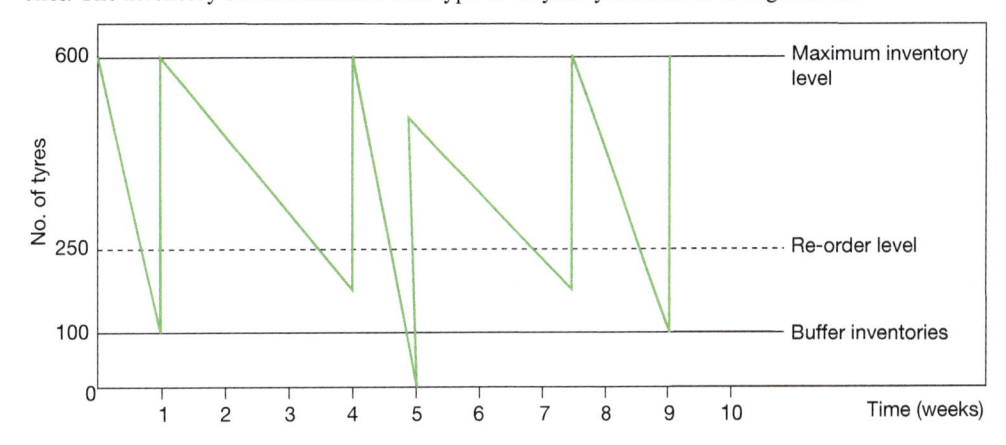

Figure 24.1 Inventory chart for one type of tyre

FBC's demand for tyres of different types from the inventory warehouse varies with output levels for different models of bicycle.

9 Is the lead time between ordering and delivery more or less than 1 week? Refer to the chart in your answer.

10 What happened during week 5?

11 Calculate the average weekly rate of inventory usage from the start of the time period (0) to the end of week 4, assuming there was an inventory of 180 tyres left at the end of week 4, assuming there was an inventory of 180 tyres left at the end of week 4.

12 Outline **two** costs to FBC of holding inventories.

13 How many tyres of this type were used during week 1?

> **WORKED EXAMPLE**
>
> 500 tyres. 600 tyres at maximum inventory level at the start of the week and this was reduced to 100 tyres (buffer inventory level) at the end of the week

Knowledge, understanding, application and analysis

The skill of analysis requires that you explain reasons for benefits and disadvantages of business decisions and the likely consequences resulting from decisions made.

14 Explain **two** costs to FBC of holding inventories of this tyre.

15 Analyse **one** advantage to FBC of holding a buffer inventory level.

16 Analyse what would have happened if delivery of this item from the supplier was not made at end of week 5.

17 Analyse **one** reason why good communication between the production department and the inventory manager is important in this case.

18 Analyse **two** benefits of FBC holding high inventories.

> **WORKED EXAMPLE**
>
> One benefit is that supply problems could occur as FBC imports the tyres and other parts **[Ap]**. Transport problems will delay delivery **[K]** especially as FBC is a long distance from a port so high inventories reduce the risk of transport problems leading to production stopping with no tyres or other parts **[An]**.

TIP
For Q19, discuss the potential advantages and disadvantages for FBC and give an overall judgement.

Knowledge, application, analysis and evaluation

The skill of evaluation requires that you make supported decisions, draw conclusions and give recommendations.

19 Discuss whether just-in-time (JIT) management of inventories should be adopted at FBC.

Exam-style questions

Paper 1

Section A

1 Define the term 'lead time'. **[2]**

2 Briefly explain two conditions necessary for JIT (just-in-time) inventory management to be effective. **[5]**

Section B

3 Analyse the importance of effective management of inventories for a manufacturing business. **[8]**

Paper 2

Spartacus Sports Shoes (SSS) (see also Chapter 23)
SSS purchases most of its supplies from local businesses but all leather used by the company is imported. Local leather is available but it is often of inferior quality and using it would damage the excellent reputation the business has for quality, customer service and prompt delivery of all orders. SSS holds high inventory levels of leather. The maximum inventory level is 40 tonnes and the buffer inventory level 10% of this amount. The economic order quantity, calculated by the SSS inventory manager, is 36 tonnes. The inventory level at which a new order is sent is 10 tonnes. This is calculated so that, taking into account the lead time of two weeks, the buffer inventory level is reached just as a new delivery arrives.

24 Inventory management

1. **a** Define the term 'economic order quantity'. **[2]**
   b Briefly explain the term 'buffer inventory level'. **[3]**
2. **a** Calculate the average weekly rate of inventory use. **[3]**
   b Comment on which costs would rise if the size of each order was reduced. **[3]**
3. Analyse the benefits to SSS of having high levels of inventories. **[8]**
4. Discuss whether SSS should adopt JIT (just-in-time) inventory management. **[11]**

Improve this answer

This is a student's answer to Q4. Skills are shown in brackets to help you.

SSS should not use JIT as it would be very risky for the business. [K] Running out of inventories would lead to a real crisis and this could put the whole business at risk. There could be many reasons why suppliers fail to deliver on time. There might be heavy traffic on the motorway or there could be a truck drivers' strike. Any problems like this would mean that the lead time is longer than usual and then inventories could fall to zero. [A] Production would have to stop, workers would have nothing to do and customers would be disappointed. These problems could damage the good name of the business and lead to customers buying products from competitors. [A] It is far too risky to use JIT so SSS should always hold high inventory levels 'just-in-case' something unforeseen happens to the next delivery.

Your challenge

See whether you can improve on this answer. It lacks direct application to SSS so no evaluation marks can be awarded. The conclusion/recommendation is not in the context of this business. A better answer is given online – but write yours out first!

25 Capacity utilisation (A Level only)

Learning outcomes

The exercises in this chapter will help you to practise what you have learnt about:

- Understanding capacity utilisation and calculating it
- Analysing the problems of excess capacity and capacity shortages
- Evaluating approaches to solving these problems
- The benefits and limitations of outsourcing.

KEY TERMS

Capacity utilisation
Excess capacity
Capacity shortage
Rationalisation

Full capacity
Outsourcing
Business process outsourcing

Key skills exercises

Knowledge and understanding

To answer the questions in this chapter, you need to know and understand:

- **the meaning and measurement of capacity utilisation**
- **capacity shortage and excess capacity and problems these cause**
- **how capacity problems might be overcome**
- **the risks and benefits of outsourcing.**

1. State the formula for calculating capacity utilisation.
2. What is meant by 'excess capacity'?
3. State **one** reason for a capacity shortage.
4. How could rationalisation reduce excess capacity?
5. State **one** disadvantage of 100% capacity working.
6. State **two** benefits of outsourcing.
7. State **two** limitations of outsourcing.

Knowledge, understanding and application

Remember to use the context provided either by the question or the data response material in your answer. One way to do this is to outline why advantages, disadvantages, benefits and limitations apply particularly to the case study business.

25 Capacity utilisation (A Level only)

Electric Appliance Company (EAC)

EAC designs and manufactures its famous brand of 'EcoHeat' electric heaters for homes and factories. It operates in a competitive market. A major rival was forced out of business recently as a result of substantial losses but many competing firms remain in the industry. EAC's fixed costs per month are $18,000.

EAC's Operations Director has collected production and output data – see Table 25.1.

	Month 1	Month 2	Month 3	This month
Production capacity (units)	12,00	1,200	1,200	1,200
Production level achieved	850	990	1,000	1,150
Capacity utilisation (%)	70.8%	82.5%	See Q8	See Q9

Table 25.1 Production and capacity utilisation levels at EAC factory

The Operations Director reported to today's Board meeting that 'this trend in capacity utilisation happened last year at about the same time. If it continues, we will be up to 100% of capacity and some customers will be disappointed. We could either extend our factory to increase capacity or outsource some production to another business.'

The Chief Executive suggested that finance was available for the factory extension but that training additional workers could be expensive. He added that outsourcing – perhaps to an overseas supplier – might give the business more flexibility.

8 Calculate capacity utilisation in month 3.

WORKED EXAMPLE

$$\text{Capacity utilisation (\%)} = \frac{\text{Current output}}{\text{Production capacity}} \times 100$$

$$= \frac{1{,}000}{1{,}200} \times 100 = 83.3\%$$

9 Calculate this month's capacity utilisation.

10 Comment on the trend in capacity utilisation.

11 Identify **two** likely causes of this trend in capacity utilisation.

12 Identify **two** risks to EAC of taking the outsourcing option.

Knowledge, understanding, application and analysis

The skill of analysis requires that you explain how or why something is an advantage or disadvantage.

13 Analyse **two** possible disadvantages to EAC of high levels of capacity working.

14 Analyse **two** possible advantages to EAC of high levels of capacity working.

Cambridge AS and A Level Business

> **WORKED EXAMPLE**
>
> One advantage to EAC of a high level of capacity utilisation is that unit costs should be quite low. **[K]** Fixed costs are $18,000 per month and when output rises from 850 to 1,150 per month, the unit fixed cost falls from $21.2 to $15.65. **[Ap]** This will make EAC much more competitive and means that the business could afford to lower prices leading to increased demand. **[A]**

> **TIP**
> For Q15, analyse the advantages and disadvantages of both ways of solving the capacity problem and make a reasoned and supported conclusion.

Knowledge, application, analysis and evaluation

The skill of evaluation requires that you make supported decisions, draw conclusions and give recommendations.

15 Discuss whether EAC should use outsourcing or extend its existing factory to solve the potential shortage of capacity problem.

Exam-style questions

Paper 3

Invictus Van Hire (IVH)

IVH operates 15 van hire centres in country X. Demand for hire vans is mainly from businesses that need additional transport capacity for short periods. Some customers are people moving house who want to do the removals themselves. The economy of country X failed to grow last year and this had the effect of cutting demand for van hire. Some van hire businesses have closed branches and reduced opening hours.

IVH have fixed costs of $450,000 per month including van leasing costs. The existing excess capacity – see Table 25.2 – is making the business much less profitable. IVH managers have been making the business more flexible in recent years. For example, they outsourced nearly all accounting work and are only appointing new employees on flexible employment contracts. However, 75% of IVH employees are still on permanent full-time contracts and trade union leaders are very keen to maintain these.

Month	1	2	3	4	5	6
Total vans available	1,100	1,100	1,100	1,100	1,100	1,100
Vans hired	600	550	600	700	770	810
Capacity utilisation %	54.5	50	54.5	63.6	70	(See Q1c)

Table 25.2 IVH: Van hire capacity and actual numbers of vans hired – current year

1 a Define the term 'excess capacity'. **[2]**
   b Briefly explain the term 'outsourcing'. **[3]**
   c Calculate the rate of capacity utilisation in month 6. **[3]**
   d Comment on the trend in capacity utilisation. **[3]**

2 Analyse the drawbacks to IVH of low levels of capacity utilisation. **[10]**

3 Discuss whether IVH should rationalise resources to reduce excess capacity. **[14]**

Improve this answer

This is a student's answer to Q3. Skills are shown in brackets to help you.

Rationalising means reducing resources in the business so that capacity is cut. [K] This will reduce the overhead or fixed costs of the business. IVH's monthly fixed costs of $450,000 [Ap] would be reduced so the losses of the business will be reduced too – or the profits increased. [A] Rationalisation in this case would cut the number of outlets. This could be done by closing one of two branches that are closest to each other. [K] Customers would still be able to hire vans from the other branch. The number of vans would have to be reduced too. So if 100 vans were sold off or returned to the leasing company, the capacity utilisation in month 6 would rise to 81% helping to reduce the average cost of each van hired out. [Ap/A]

Workers would probably have to be made redundant when one or more branches close and this will further reduce costs. [K] This might upset the Trade Union and they might call industrial action. This might be unlikely though as the economy is not doing very well and the Trade Union would worry about IVH having to close even more branches. [A] IVH might be able to avoid redundancy if they introduced more flexible labour contracts for existing workers as these would cut back on fixed costs too as the hours of each worker could be reduced. [Ap/A/E]

Your challenge

See whether you can improve on this answer – which does have some important strengths. It seems to lack one very important part of a successful 'discuss' answer. There is no overall, supported conclusion. A better answer is given online – but write yours out first.

management (A Level only)

Learning outcomes

The exercises in this chapter will help you to practise what you have learnt about:

- The importance of lean production including the main lean production techniques
- Defining quality and evaluating the differences between quality control and quality assurance
- Quality assurance and Total Quality Management (TQM)
- The link between quality and business competitiveness
- The importance of benchmarking and how it is undertaken.

KEY TERMS

Lean production	Quality assurance
Simultaneous engineering	ISO 9000
Cell production	Total Quality Management (TQM)
Kaizen	Internal customers
Quality product	Zero defects
Quality standards	Benchmarking
Quality control	

Key skills exercises

Knowledge and understanding

To answer the questions in this chapter, you need to know and understand:

- **the concept of lean production and links to inventory control and capacity management**
- **techniques that businesses can use to help achieve lean production**
- **the meaning and significance of quality**
- **the contrasting approaches to achieving quality products.**

1. State **one** aim of lean production.
2. How does simultaneous engineering save resources?
3. How can 'flexibility' in production achieve greater efficiency?
4. Explain the term 'kaizen'.
5. State **three** claimed benefits of lean production.
6. State **three** situations in which lean production might not be appropriate.
7. What is meant by the term 'quality product'?
8. Differentiate between 'quality control' and 'quality assurance'.
9. Explain the term 'Total Quality Management'.
10. State one purpose of benchmarking.

26 Lean production and quality management (A Level only)

Knowledge, understanding and application

Remember to use the context provided either by the question or the data response material in your answer. One way to do this is to outline why advantages and disadvantages apply particularly to the case study business.

> ### Electric Appliance Company (EAC) (see also Chapter 25)
>
> As output has increased and capacity utilisation approached 100%, some significant problems started to arise within the factory. These were:
>
> - no space in the warehouse for the additional inventories of components needed for higher production levels
> - increased number of faulty products being rejected by quality inspectors
> - delays in production caused by increased employee absenteeism – other workers are not able to perform the jobs of the workers who were absent
> - increased complaints from employees – they are being asked to work harder but are not involved in solving problems that could make production more efficient.
>
> The Chief Executive is becoming worried about delays in the development and launch of the new model of EcoHeat appliance. This was planned to be ready for marketing last year but the launch has just been delayed another three months. He told other directors, 'Although demand is high at present, our lack of new models will affect us greatly in future. Unless our employees in all departments – including Research and Development – solve these problems, we will have to make clear to them that the consequences will be the loss of their jobs.'
>
> The Operations Director replied, 'I have been suggesting for some time now that we need to adopt lean production principles and Total Quality Management. These changes will require some investment in machines and training as well as a different style of leadership.'

11 Outline **three** examples of 'waste' within EAC that results from not adopting lean production.

> **WORKED EXAMPLE**
>
> One example of waste in EAC is the use of expensive storage space and the opportunity costs associated with this resulting from high inventory levels. **[K]** At EAC there is 'no more space in the warehouse' as rising output led to more components held in inventory. **[Ap]**

12 Outline **two** reasons why the consequences of low quality are becoming more serious.

13 Suggest **two** possible links between low employee motivation and the problems that EAC's Operation department is experiencing.

14 Does EAC seem to be using 'quality control' or 'quality assurance'? Explain your answer.

Knowledge, understanding, application and analysis

The skill of analysis requires that you explain 'why' or 'how' something is a 'benefit' or drawback.

15 Analyse **two** disadvantages to EAC of not adopting lean production techniques.

16 Analyse the potential advantages to EAC of adopting:
  a simultaneous engineering
  b Kaizen.

17 Analyse **two** disadvantages of EAC not adopting the quality assurance approach.

> **WORKED EXAMPLE**
>
> In focussing on quality control EAC employs quality control inspectors. **[K]** There has been an increase in the number of faulty products identified by these inspectors. **[Ap]** As employees are not held responsible for quality and there appear to be no quality assurance standards, the cost of increased numbers of faulty products is rising. **[A]**

Knowledge, application, analysis and evaluation

The skill of evaluation requires that you make supported decisions, draw conclusions and give recommendations.

18 Discuss whether EAC should adopt the principle of lean production.

> **TIP**
>
> For Q18, analyse the benefits of some lean production techniques for EAC (would it lead to increased output without spending money on a factory extension?). Then analyse some of the potential limitations, for example cost (could the business afford to train for lean production techniques to be introduced at same time as a factory extension?). Finally, give a supported conclusion/decision.

19 Evaluate **two** approaches to lean production that EAC could adopt.

20 Discuss whether Total Quality Management would be appropriate for EAC.

Exam-style questions

Paper 3

Resort Spa Hotels (RSH)

RSH operates 30 luxury hotels. Managing quality of customer service at RSH used to be based on quality control checks by supervisors. For example, the Head of Housekeeping used to check a sample of rooms that had been cleaned, the Catering Manager sampled recipes devised by the chefs and 'secret clients' monitored the length of time taken to check in and out of the hotels. Employee motivation was low and labour turnover high. Three years ago a new Chief Executive introduced Total Quality Management. She insisted that all employees should have responsibility for quality of customer service. Clear and measurable assurance standards were set for as many hotel activities as possible and employees were encouraged to check their own performance

26 Lean production and quality management (A Level only)

against these. Combined with an effective performance-related pay scheme, customer complaints fell by 75%, employee absenteeism was halved and labour turnover reduced.

Although hotel costs have fallen as a result of TQM – despite the additional training required – the Chief Executive is now determined to make RSH much leaner and more efficient. In a recent benchmarking exercise, RSH did not do well on cost and price competitiveness and had a higher level of wastage of food and drink than the best in the industry. RSH plans to introduce lean production techniques in all of its hotels to cut waste and costs and to improve labour productivity.

1. Analyse how the introduction of Total Quality Management achieved the benefits outlined in the case study. **[10]**
2. Discuss whether any **two** lean production techniques, if introduced at RSH, are likely to reduce costs and improve efficiency. **[14]**

Improve this answer

This is a student's answer to Q2. Skills are shown in brackets to help you.

Lean production means reducing waste in all areas of production whilst maintaining quality. [K] Waste can occur in manufacturing, e.g. too many faulty products, but it can also occur in hotels. For example, food and drink can be wasted if over-ordered and allowed to go past its 'use by date'. [Ap] Low productivity in cleaning rooms, preparing food, checking out clients and so on can waste labour resources. [Ap] Lack of flexibility amongst employees can mean that when a worker is absent, such as a lobby porter, no one is available to do the job. [Ap]

Lean production at RSH could include JIT and flexible working. [K] With JIT, only sufficient food and drink will be held in inventory to meet immediate needs. Inventories will only be sufficient to cover the time period of re-ordering and delivery. This will save on costs of inventory holding, reduce opportunity costs of finance held in inventory and help to keep food as fresh as possible. [Ap] This will improve the customer's experience in the restaurants of the hotels as well as reducing costs. [A]

Flexible working requires a multi-skilled workforce which is prepared to undertake a variety of different jobs in the hotel. This will mean that no one should be left idle, no vacancies caused by absenteeism left uncovered by someone else and really busy periods, such as in the kitchen, will have extra workers available to help. A smaller number of employees will be required and labour productivity will increase. Employees may feel more motivated due to the team-working spirit that this system encourages and by the variety of being able to undertake a large number of different jobs. [A]

Your challenge

See whether you can improve this answer – which does have some important strengths such as being well applied to 'hotels'. It seems to lack one very important 'skill' – there is no overall evaluation of whether lean production will 'reduce costs and improve efficiency'. The answer is too one-sided – there is no analysis of the potential cost/limitations of these lean production techniques. A better answer is given online – but write yours out first!

27 Project management (A Level only)

Learning outcomes

The exercises in this chapter will help you to practise what you have learnt about:

- The need for project management and why some projects fail
- The main elements of a network diagram and construct a diagram
- Using critical path analysis (CPA) and evaluating this approach to project management.

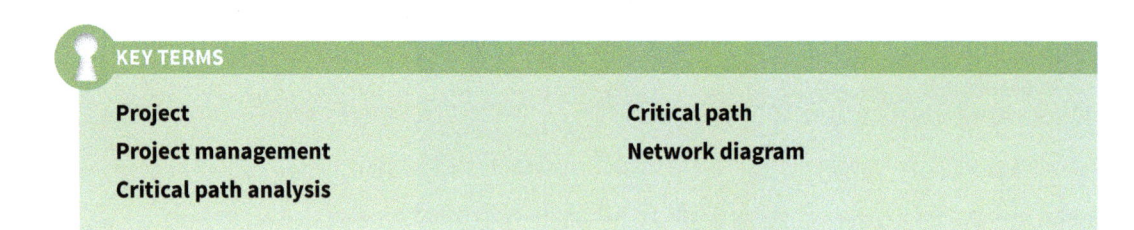

KEY TERMS

Project
Project management
Critical path analysis
Critical path
Network diagram

Key skills exercises

Knowledge and understanding

To answer the questions in this chapter, you need to know and understand:
- **the importance of managing new projects effectively**
- **the use of network diagrams including their construction**
- **critical path analysis.**

1 State **three** of the key elements of a project.

2 State **three** possible reasons for the failure of a project to build a new power station (apart from lack of finance).

3 Suggest **two** consequences for the construction business building the power station.

4 What **three** pieces of information do the nodes on a network diagram display?

5 State the formula for 'total float'.

6 State the formula for 'free float'.

7 Give **one** potential benefit of knowing the total float of an activity.

8 Define the term 'critical path'.

9 State **two** advantages of CPA.

10 State **two** limitations of CPA.

27 Project management (A Level only)

Knowledge, understanding and application

Remember to use the context provided either by the question or the data response material in your answer. One way to do this is to outline why advantages and disadvantages apply particularly to the case study business.

New City Hospital (NCH)

NCH plans to demolish its accident and emergency department and build a new one. This project must be completed within 30 weeks. This is the length of the lease that NCH has taken out on alternative accommodation while the project is undertaken. Also, if accident and emergency services are not offered to the high standard expected by the government after 30 weeks, NCH managers have been threatened with dismissal. NCH has its own project manager. She has drawn up the main activities to be undertaken during this project. She will contract builders and specialists at key times during the project based on the times shown in Table 27.1. They must all complete their activities in the times shown.

Activity	Details	Duration (weeks)	Preceding activities
A	Remove existing equipment	2	–
B	Order new equipment and await delivery	9	–
C	Recruit additional medical staff	2	–
D	Demolish old building	4	A
E	Select additional medical staff	3	C
F	Construct new building	12	D
G	Decorate new building	4	F
H	Install new equipment	3	G, B
I	Train all medical staff on new equipment	3	H, E
J	Test all systems	1	I

Table 27.1 Main activities for the construction of the new NCH accident and emergency department.

11 Draw the network diagram using the information in Table 27.1.

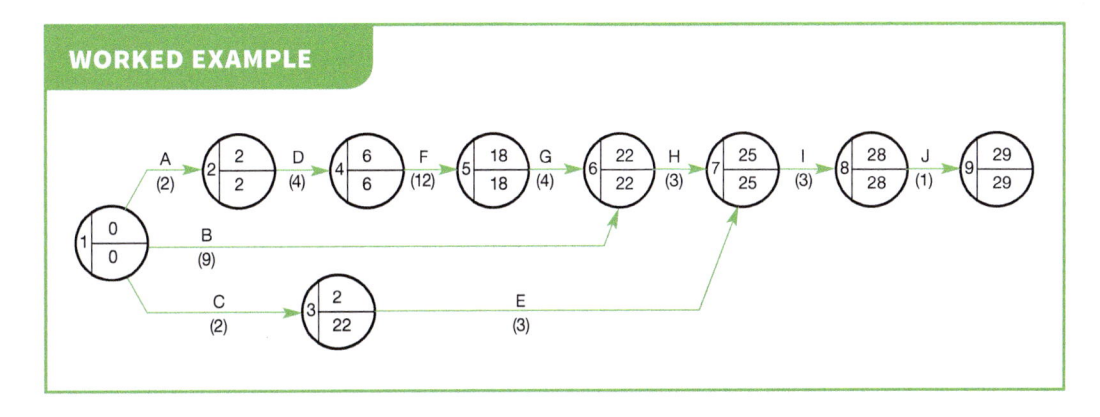

WORKED EXAMPLE

Cambridge AS and A Level Business

12 Insert the earliest start times and latest finish times into the nodes.

13 Identify the critical path.

14 Calculate total float times on B and E.

15 Outline what would happen if activity F took two weeks longer than planned.

16 How might the problem identified in Q15 be overcome?

17 Will the project be completed within 30 weeks, according to this CPA?

> **TIP**
> For Q20, refer to the actual network diagram, the likelihood of all activities keeping to time, the lack of experience of the project manager and any other factors that might influence the outcome of this project. Remember to include a clear, supported conclusion.

Knowledge, understanding, application and analysis

The skill of analysis requires that you explain 'why' or 'how' something is a 'benefit or drawback.

18 Analyse two advantages of using CPA in this case.

19 Analyse two limitations of the CPA in this case.

Knowledge, application, analysis and evaluation

The skill of evaluation requires that you make supported decisions, draw conclusions and give recommendations.

20 Discuss whether the new accident and emergency building will be completed within 30 weeks.

Exam-style questions

Paper 3

High Quality (HQ) – an online marketing project

HQ is a well-known chain of food supermarkets. It operates from 120 locations throughout the country. It is experiencing increasing competition from 'discount' retailers and businesses that sell food and other household requirements online. The directors of HQ have decided to launch a new website that will allow online ordering of all of the 8,000 different items found in one of the HQ supermarkets. Delivery 'within four hours' is going to be promised by the company. Many new trucks will be needed and over 100 drivers will need to be recruited. The directors plan for the new website and transport team to be ready for a huge national launch of the project in six months' time. It is by far the largest IT project HQ has ever attempted and the directors, to save on costs, have decided that all development of the website and the online ordering system will be done 'in-house' and not be outsourced to specialist businesses. The schedule of the major activities is shown in Table 27.2.

Activity	Duration (weeks)	Preceding activities
A	2	–
B	5	A
C	7	A
D	5	A
E	4	D
F	3	B, C, E
G	6	F
H	4	F
I	1	G, H
J	3	I

Table 27.2 Major activities for the HQ online selling project

1 a i Draw the network diagram for the project. **[6]**

   ii Insert all ESTs and LFTs. **[4]**

   b Discuss the usefulness of CPA in managing this project. **[12]**

Annotate this answer

This is a student's answer to Q1b.

CPA is a planning technique that uses a network diagram of project activities. The CP is made up of activities A, D, E, F, G, I and J. The length of this critical path is 24 weeks, which is just less than the 6 months' target time. This suggests that the project should be completed in time for the launch of the online selling of HQ products. If there is a delay in any of the critical activities – such as D for example – then this might extend the completion time to over 6 months. In this case, more resources would need to be devoted to one of the later critical activities such as G to reduce the estimated duration time. In this way the completion time could be kept down to 6 months. It might be possible to switch some employee resources from one of the activities with a float time, such as H, to help complete G in less than the estimated duration time.

The CP analysis and the network diagram will help HQ complete this project on time. It shows the main activities, the logical relationship between them and the critical activities. These must be focused on by the project team within HQ to try to make sure that the durations are not exceeded. Using the diagram allows resources to be switched from non-critical to critical activities, as explained above.

The CP analysis and the diagram will not guarantee success of this project or its completion within 6 months, however. This is a 'one-off' project, not undertaken by HQ before, and there might be considerable inaccuracies in the estimated duration times. The project is also larger than anything HQ has attempted before, in terms of IT. It could be that the IT employees in the business are just not capable of managing such a complex project and it might have been wiser to outsource this to IT specialists, even though this would have been more expensive.

On balance, I think there are too many uncertainties about this project and HQ's ability to manage it. Yes, the CP analysis and the network diagram will be useful in the ways analysed but only up to a point. What would be much more useful is a skilled externally appointed IT expert with knowledge of this type of project to help manage and see it through to completion within 6 months.

Your challenge

This time you have been provided with a really good answer! Your challenge is to read through it carefully and annotate it with the four skills (K, Ap, A and E). This has been done online – but make sure you annotate your own copy first!

Unit 4 Research task

Tata Motors to improve efficiency

Guenter Butschek, the recently appointed Chief Executive of Tata Motors, is planning to introduce crucial operational changes including the company's manufacturing processes to make the company more flexible and responsive to market trends. The CEO said his focus would be to make the company leaner and more flexible, which will help it respond faster to market changes than it has historically. 'We will identify the root causes of some of the inefficiencies we experience at Tata Motors. You need to be sufficiently agile and fast in responding to consumer demand and processes need to be simpler.'

The company will focus on technology, design and quality for the next three models which will be introduced shortly – the Tiago, Hexa and Nexon. These models will allow customers to select a wide range of colours and extras as the production methods will be made more flexible.

Tata will also cut down on the number of suppliers in order to improve communication, quality and consistency. The overall aim of these measures is to increase productivity and to keep Tata one of the most competitive of car manufacturers in Asia.

Adapted from Business-Standard.com

Write a report to Tata Motors CEO – or the CEO of any large manufacturing business in your country – explaining:

1. The importance of using operational management to maintain competitiveness.

2. The changes that could be made to the company's operations (production methods, capacity levels, inventory management etc) to increase productivity and competitiveness.

Unit 5
Finance and accounting

28 Business finance

Learning outcomes

The exercises in this chapter will help you to practise what you have learnt about:

- Why businesses need finance (e.g. for start-up and expansion)
- Understanding working capital and analysing its importance
- Differentiating between short- and long-term, and internal and external, sources of finance
- The advantages and disadvantages of different sources of finance
- Making informed decisions about the most suitable sources of finance in different business situations
- The factors managers consider when taking a finance decision.

KEY TERMS

Start-up capital	Leasing
Working capital	Equity (share) finance
Capital expenditure	Long-term loans
Revenue expenditure	Long-term bonds or debentures
Liquidity	Rights issue
Liquidation	Venture capital
Overdraft	Microfinance
Factoring	Crowd funding
Hire purchase	Business plan

Key skills exercises

Knowledge and understanding

To answer the questions in this chapter, you need to know and understand:

- **reasons why businesses need finance**
- **capital expenditure and revenue expenditure**
- **internal and external sources of finance**
- **factors that influence the finance decision.**

1. State **two** reasons why a new internet café will require finance.
2. Define 'working capital'.
3. How can working capital be used as a source of finance?
4. Differentiate between capital expenditure by a business and revenue expenditure.
5. Why might a business be 'liquidated' if it has no working capital?
6. Differentiate between a bank loan and an overdraft.
7. State **one** advantage of leasing fixed assets.
8. What is meant by the term 'rights issue'?

9 State **two** ways in which a public limited company can sell additional shares.

10 Is a sale of shares an example of internal or external finance?

11 Define 'venture capital'.

12 Define 'microfinance'.

13 Give **one** advantage of microfinance schemes to business start-ups in low-income countries.

14 What is meant by the term 'crowd funding'?

15 State **one** advantage of crowd funding for a new business start-up.

16 Why is the 'size of existing borrowing' important to a manager when considering taking out a further loan.

17 Why is factoring considered a short-term source of finance?

18 Differentiate between 'hire purchase' and 'leasing' of equipment.

19 Suggest **one** advantage to a business of receiving a government grant.

20 Suggest **one** relationship between the legal structure of a business and its main sources of finance.

Knowledge, understanding and application

Remember to apply your answers to finance questions to the case study business. For example, suggesting that a small start-up business should use a 'public issue of shares' to raise capital is obviously inappropriate.

'Brightest and Best Cleaning' (BBC)

Jason set up his home cleaning business, BBC, two years ago. He offers cleaning services to householders in his town and in the local area. He used his own savings to start up the business. He bought a cheap van and a large electric household floor cleaner. He uses the best cleaning materials available as he wants to establish a reputation as being the 'brightest and best cleaning service for your home'.

He is a sole trader despite having expanded his business by employing three workers. One keeps the accounts and answers the telephone at the very small office and store area for cleaning materials that Jason now rents near his home. The other two workers help Jason clean homes quickly. Jason makes a profit from his business and he wants to expand it further by buying a second van and renting a larger store room. He thinks an overdraft would be the best source of finance to use.

21 Outline **two** benefits to Jason of using 'own savings' to start up the business.

22 Why could Jason not sell shares to raise finance?

23 Outline, using examples from the case study, the difference between capital expenditure and revenue expenditure.

28 Business finance

> **WORKED EXAMPLE**
>
> Capital expenditure is on assets that last for more than one year. **[K]** The vans and electric cleaners last for more than one year. **[Ap]**
>
> Revenue expenditure is on costs or assets that last less than one year. **[K]** In this case, it includes cleaning materials and cleaner's wages. **[Ap]**

24 Outline **one** disadvantage to Jason of using an overdraft to finance business expansion.

25 Suggest **two** sources of finance, other than an overdraft, that Jason could use to pay for the expansion of the business.

26 Are the sources you have suggested in Q25, internal or external sources?

27 Outline **one** disadvantage to Jason of each of the sources suggested in Q25.

Knowledge, understanding, application and analysis

Explaining the benefits and drawbacks of different sources of finance or the 'factors that managers should consider before arranging finance' are all common forms of analysis required in this section of the syllabus.

> Jason expanded the business by using his savings from the first two years of operation and a small bank loan. BBC's cleaning services are very popular and some customers have asked Jason if he cleans offices too.
>
> Jason has decided to expand into office cleaning. To offer a reliable service all year round he has calculated that he will need three more vans, a small crane to access windows in high office buildings, more cleaning machines and additional employees. He has discussed his plans with a bank manager who explained the finance options Jason has. Some of them would require him to change the legal structure of his business.

28 Analyse **two** benefits to Jason of selling shares in his business by converting it into a limited company.

> **WORKED EXAMPLE**
>
> One benefit for Jason of selling shares is that capital will be raised **[K]** which is permanent and will not have to be repaid. **[An]** BBC will not have to repay the amount raised. **[Ap]**

29 Analyse **two** factors that might discourage Jason from taking out further loans to expand the business.

30 Analyse **two** reasons why a bank might be unwilling to give Jason a big loan without a detailed business plan for his expansion.

Cambridge AS and A Level Business

> **TIP**
> For Q31, consider what Jason will need the finance for; analyse the advantages and disadvantages of two or three sources of finance; make a supported final recommendation.

WORKED EXAMPLE

Reason 1: A big loan implies a large risk for the bank **[K]** – the bank will want reassurance from a business plan that Jason has thought carefully about how much capital he needs and what he intends to spend it on especially as BBC is still quite a small business. **[An/Ap]**

Knowledge, application, analysis and evaluation

The skill of evaluation requires that you make supported decisions, draw conclusions and give recommendations.

31 Recommend to Jason which sources of finance to use for the business expansion. Justify your recommendation.

Exam-style questions

Paper 1

Section A

1 Explain **three** sources of finance available to a sole trader. **[5]**
2 Differentiate, with examples, between short- and long-term sources of finance. **[3]**

Section B

3 Discuss the factors the directors of a public limited company should consider before taking decisions about additional long-term sources of finance. **[20]**

Paper 2

Terrafirma Transport (TT)

TT is a public limited company. It used to be owned by the Sarlat family and the family still owns 40% of the shares. TT operates daily bus routes in country X and offers bus hire to groups and schools. It also operates employee transport for large companies that need their workers to arrive at work on time. Several years ago, TT was in financial difficulties. Debts increased and it was owed huge sums by business customers who had taken longer to pay than expected. The directors arranged a sale of assets that were considered not to be essential to the company. Since then, managed by Sami, the new Chief Executive Officer, TT has just started to become profitable and now there are plans to expand. Sami wants to double the number of buses to be used mainly for employee transport contracts. Some buses will be leased and others bought as Sami has been offered a discounted price by one bus manufacturer. Two new TT depots will be needed, each with their own fuel and spare parts inventories. He has not yet decided on whether to use share capital or take out an additional long-term loan to finance the expansion.

28 Business finance

1. **a** Define the term 'sale of assets'. **[2]**
   b Briefly explain the term 'share capital'. **[3]**
2. Outline **two** benefits to TT of leasing some of the additional buses. **[6]**
3. Analyse **two** reasons why TT will need to increase its working capital when it expands. **[8]**
4. Recommend to TT's directors whether to take out a further loan or sell additional shares to finance TT's expansion. **[11]**

Improve this answer

This is a student's answer to Q3. Skills are shown in brackets to help you.

Working capital is the finance needed for the day to day operation of the business. [K] It is used to buy inventories and pay bills. It is also needed for the materials used and wages paid in making products that are sold on credit – before customers pay for them.

An expanding business will usually need to hold more inventories of materials. [K] These will need to be financed so increasing the need for working capital.

Secondly, expanding businesses need more customers. [An] Many customers demand credit terms before buying products, especially expensive ones. By making products, selling them but not being paid for them yet requires additional working capital finance. [An]

Your challenge

This is an accurate answer, showing good understanding and some analysis but it is not applied to TT. See whether you can improve this answer. A better one is available on line – but write yours out first!

29 Costs

Learning outcomes

The exercises in this chapter will help you to practise what you have learnt about:

- Understanding the types of costs – how costs are classified
- Analysing the need for and uses of accurate cost data
- Using accurate cost data – pricing, business decisions and measuring business performance
- Using break-even charts and calculations to analyse business performance and the impact of business decisions
- Evaluating break-even analysis.

KEY TERMS

Direct costs
Indirect costs
Fixed costs
Variable costs

Marginal costs
Break-even point of production
Margin of safety
Contribution per unit

Key skills exercises

Knowledge and understanding

To answer the questions in this chapter, you need to know and understand:

- **cost classifications**
- **why some costs vary with output and others do not**
- **the key features of a break-even chart and calculation.**

1. State **three** reasons why managers need accurate cost information.
2. Differentiate between direct and indirect costs.
3. Differentiate between fixed and variable costs.
4. Explain whether a direct cost can also be a fixed cost.
5. Differentiate between marginal cost and average cost.
6. What is meant by the 'break-even level of production'?
7. What will happen to the break-even point if fixed costs increase but all other costs and price remain unchanged?
8. Define 'safety margin' (or 'margin of safety').
9. State the break-even formula.
10. If the contribution per unit increases, what will happen to the break-even level of production?

29 Costs

Knowledge, understanding and application

Remember to apply your answers to cost questions to the case study business. For example, the variable costs of a nuclear power station will be very different from the variable costs of a sweet shop!

Seaport Hotel (SH)

SH is a luxury hotel with 300 bedrooms. The hotel has a large gymnasium and swimming pool that can be used by non-residents. There are several conference rooms, which are popular with local businesses for seminars, meetings and large conferences. There are separate divisions in the hotel, all headed by a sub-manager: accommodation, restaurants, conferences, gymnasium and swimming pool. The General Manager of the hotel, Leo, is worried about the low profitability of the conference division. He has asked the Sub-Manager of the conference division for some recent cost, price and demand data (see Table 29.1)

Variable cost per conference delegate per day (food, drinks etc)	$30
Weekly fixed costs of conference division	$21,000
Average number of delegates per week (attending for 1 day each)	320
Price charged to businesses per delegate per day	$100

Table 29.1 Data for conference division

'We could increase the daily price per delegate by 5% to improve profitability,' said the Conference Manager. 'Yes, or we could save 10% per delegate on cheaper food and drinks,' replied Leo, 'or increase our advertising fixed costs and try to increase the number of delegates by 20 each week. We need to take one of these decisions to improve the profitability of this division.'

11 Give **two** examples of direct costs for the conference division.

12 Are the direct costs you have identified in Q11 also variable costs? Explain your answer.

13 Give **two** examples of fixed costs for a hotel.

14 Calculate total weekly cost of the conference division if there were 350 delegates attending for 1 day each.

15 Calculate average cost at this output level.

16 Calculate the break-even number of delegates each week (attending for 1 day).

WORKED EXAMPLE

$$\text{Break-even} = \frac{\text{Fixed costs}}{\text{Contribution per unit}}$$

$$= \frac{\$21{,}000}{(\$100 - \$30)}$$

= 300 delegates per week (for one day each)

17 Calculate the break-even number of delegates following Leo's proposed price increase.

18 Comment on your results to Q16 and Q17 and refer to margin of safety in your answer.

Cambridge AS and A Level Business

Knowledge, understanding, application and analysis

Explaining the benefits and drawbacks of techniques such as break-even analysis is an important example of analysis.

19 Analyse **two** ways in which the Conference Manager could use the cost information provided.

20 Explain **one** reason why the Production Manager would find it useful to understand the difference between fixed and variable costs.

21 Analyse **two** limitations to break-even analysis in this case.

> **WORKED EXAMPLE**
>
> One limitation in this case is that the variable cost line is a straight line because the cost of $30 per delegate for food and drink is constant. **[K/Ap]** It might be possible, with a larger number of delegates to obtain economies of bulk purchasing, in which case the variable cost line would not be of a constant gradient – and neither would the total cost line. **[An]** This would reduce the break-even number of delegates needed to break-even. **[Ap/An]**

22 Analyse why the marginal cost of providing services to an additional delegate would be less than the average cost.

Knowledge, application, analysis and evaluation

The skill of evaluation requires that you make supported decisions, draw conclusions and give recommendations.

23 Recommend, using break-even analysis, which decision should be taken for improving the profitability of the conference division. Justify your recommendation.

> **TIP**
> For Q23, analyse the impact of the three different decisions that could be taken by calculating break-even point, weekly profit and safety margin. Using your results, recommend which decision to take – at the same time, identifying the limitations of break-even analysis.

Exam-style questions

Paper 1

Section A

1 Give an example of **one** variable cost and one fixed cost for a petrol station. Explain your choice. **[3]**

2 Explain **one** benefit to a production manager of using break-even charts. **[5]**

Section B

3 a Analyse why it is important for a business that makes several products to differentiate between direct and indirect costs. **[8]**

   b Evaluate the usefulness of break-even analysis to a retail business that operates several shops. **[12]**

Paper 2

Tariq's Wooden Toys (TWT)

Tariq's hobby was making toys. He has now turned his hobby into a profitable business. He employs four skilled craft workers who are paid above the average wage rate. His products are sold online to customers all over the world. He designs the toys himself – puppets, trains and dinosaurs are the best-selling items. His latest design was launched last year – it is a large dragon painted in bright colours. Sales have been disappointing and last month, TWT made a small profit for the first time on this toy by selling 300 units. A monthly break-even chart is shown in Figure 29.1.

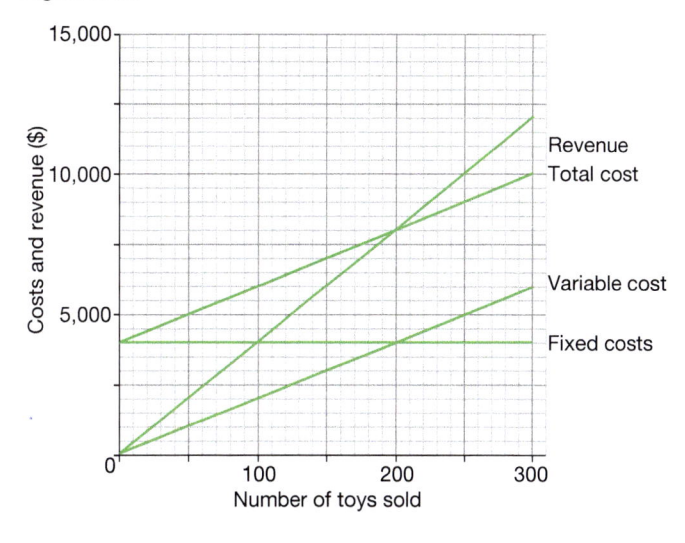

Figure 29.1 TWT monthly break-even chart

The Production Manager explained to Tariq that the variable costs of this particular toy were high as it used a lot of special paints and was time consuming to make. A version that was easier to make and less colourful had been rejected by the directors of TWT last year. It also needed a specialised tool to make it that could not be used on other toys. The Production Manager suggested that the indirect costs that the dragon was expected to pay for were too high. Tariq suggested raising the price to $50 per toy. He asked for this to be shown on the break-even chart.

1. a Define 'variable cost'. **[2]**
   b Briefly explain the term 'indirect cost'. **[3]**
2. a i Add to the break-even chart a new revenue line based on $50 per toy. **[2]**
      ii Show clearly the new safety margin, assuming monthly sales of 300 units. **[1]**
   b Comment on this revised break-even chart. **[3]**
3. Analyse two ways, other than the price increase suggested by Tariq, which could be used to try to reduce the break-even level of production. **[8]**
4. Discuss the usefulness of break-even analysis when making decisions that aim to improve the profitability of the dragon toy. **[11]**

Improve this answer

This is a student's answer to Q3.

The break-even level of production depends not just on price but also variable and fixed costs – which add up to total costs.

One way to reduce the break-even point and increase profit is to reduce labour costs. These are likely to be variable costs and a reduction in wages will make the variable cost line on the break-even chart rise less steeply. As total costs also depend on variable costs, this line will rise less steeply too, meaning that it crosses the revenue line (break-even point) at a lower level of production.

Another way to reduce the break-even point is to reduce fixed costs. This could be done by moving to a cheaper factory and cutting rent costs. This will lower the horizontal fixed-cost line and total costs will fall too. By reducing total cost, the line will cut the revenue line at a lower output level. This reduces the break-even level of production.

Your challenge

This is another accurate answer, showing good understanding and some analysis but it is not applied to TWT. There is no reference to 'above average wages' or 'special paints' or 'high indirect costs' – all mentioned in the case study. The student avoids wasting time by NOT evaluating the points made as it was only an 'analyse' question. See whether you can improve this answer. A better one is available on line – but write yours out first!

30 Accounting fundamentals

Learning outcomes

The exercises in this chapter will help you to practise what you have learnt about:

- The importance of accounting records
- The main users of accounts and their need for accounting information
- The main components of an income statement
- The main components of a statement of financial position
- Analysing business accounts by using liquidity and profitability ratios
- The limitations of ratio analysis and published accounts.

KEY TERMS

Income statement	Current assets
Gross profit	Inventories
Revenue	Trade receivables (debtors)
Cost of sales	Current liabilities
Operating profit	Accounts payable (creditors)
Profit for the year	Non-current liabilities
Dividends	Intellectual capital or property
Retained earnings	Goodwill
Low-quality profit	Cash-flow statement
High-quality profit	Gross profit margin
Statement of financial position	Operating (net profit) margin
Shareholders' equity	Liquidity
Share capital	Current ratio
Asset	Acid test ratio
Liability	Liquid assets
Non-current assets	Window dressing
Intangible assets	

Key skills exercises

Knowledge and understanding

To answer the questions in this chapter, you need to know and understand:

- the uses of accounting data
- the key items recorded on an income statement
- the key items recorded on a statement of financial position
- liquidity and profit margin ratios.

1. State **three** reasons why managers need to keep accurate accounting records.
2. List **three** stakeholder groups interested in a company's accounts.
3. Suggest **one** reason why each group in Q2 is interested in these accounts.
4. Define the term 'cost of sales'.

5 What is the key difference between 'gross profit' and 'operating profit'?
6 All other things remaining constant, how would an increase in dividends impact on retained earnings? Explain your answer.
7 Is the expression 'For the year ending' usually found on an income statement or a statement of financial position? Explain your answer.
8 Using examples, differentiate between an asset and a liability.
9 Using examples, differentiate between a tangible non-current asset and an intangible asset.
10 Which current asset is not included in 'liquid assets' when calculating the acid test ratio – and why?
11 Is 'Accounts payable' an asset or a liability?
12 Give **one** example of a non-current liability.
13 Give **one** example of a current liability.
14 State **two** items usually recorded in 'Shareholders' equity'.
15 State **two** ways in which a business might attempt to increase its gross profit margin in future.
16 Explain why the current ratio result is always higher than the acid test ratio.
17 State **one** way in which a business could improve its acid test ratio result.
18 State **two** possible limitations of ratio results.
19 State **two** possible limitations of published accounts.
20 Suggest **one** reason why it might be important to compare profit margin results with another company in the same industry.

Knowledge, understanding and application

Remember to apply your answers to cost questions to the case study business and to use the appropriate data when calculating ratio results.

Seaport Hotel (see also Chapter 29)

Leo wants to assess the performance and liquidity of the hotel. The economy is in recession and a large hotel group has just gone out of business. Leo believes that SH is liquid and profitable enough to survive but he has asked the hotel's accountant for key financial data. They will then undertake ratio analysis to assess the hotel's performance and liquidity. This is shown in Table 30.1.

	2017	2016
Annual revenue	5	5.2
Cost of sales	4	3.8
Operating profit	0.2	0.6
Inventories	1	0.8
Cash in bank and hotel	0.2	0.6
Accounts receivable	0.5	0.6
Current liabilities	2	1.6

Table 30.1 Key financial data for Seaport Hotel ($m)

21 Calculate the gross profit margin for 2016.

> **WORKED EXAMPLE**
>
> Gross profit = Revenue − Cost of sales = $1.4m
>
> GP margin % = (Gross profit/Revenue) × 100
>
> $= \dfrac{\$1.4m}{\$5.2m} \times 100 = 26.9\%$

22 Calculate the gross profit margin for 2017.

23 Comment on the results to Q21 and Q22.

24 Calculate the operating profit margin for 2016.

> **WORKED EXAMPLE**
>
> Operating profit margin % = (Operating profit/Revenue) × 100
>
> $= \dfrac{\$0.6m}{\$5.2m} \times 100 = 11.5\%$

25 Calculate the operating profit margin for 2017.

26 Comment on the results to Q24 and Q25.

27 Suggest **two** factors that might have caused the trends in these profit margin results.

28 Calculate the current ratio for 2016.

> **WORKED EXAMPLE**
>
> Current ratio = $\dfrac{\text{Current assets (inventories + cash + accounts receivable)}}{\text{Current liabilities}}$
>
> $= \dfrac{\$2m}{\$1.6m} = 1.25$

29 Calculate the current ratio for 2017.

30 Comment on the results for Q28 and Q29.

31 Calculate the acid test ratio for 2016.

> **WORKED EXAMPLE**
>
> Acid test = $\dfrac{\text{Liquid assets}}{\text{Current liabilities}}$
>
> $= \dfrac{\$1.2m}{\$1.6m} = 0.75$

32 Calculate the acid test ratio for 2017.

33 Comment on the results to Q31 and Q32.

34 Suggest **two** factors that might have caused the trends in the liquidity ratios.

Knowledge, understanding, application and analysis

Explaining the benefits and drawbacks of different sources of finance or the factors that managers should consider before arranging finance are all common forms of analysis required in this section of the syllabus.

35 Analyse **two** reasons for the declining profitability at SH.

36 Analyse **two** possible problems that might result from this decline in profitability.

37 Analyse **two** benefits to Leo of undertaking this ratio analysis.

38 Analyse **two** reasons for the changes in SH's liquidity.

39 Analyse **two** ways in which SH's liquidity could be improved.

TIP
For Q40, analyse the uses to which these ratio results can be put but also consider the limitations e.g. are enough years' results being used?

Knowledge, application, analysis and evaluation

The skill of evaluation requires that you make supported decisions, draw conclusions and give recommendations. Explaining the ratio results, the benefits and limitations of ratio analysis and explaining how ratio results might be improved are all important forms of analysis in this section.

40 Evaluate the usefulness of Leo's ratio analysis using the data in Table 30.1.

41 Recommend to Leo ways in which the profit margins of SH could be improved.

Exam-style questions

Paper 1

Section A

1 Differentiate between gross profit and retained earnings. **[3]**

2 Explain two limitations of the published accounts of a limited company. **[5]**

Section B

3 a Analyse why any two stakeholders in a limited company will be interested in its published accounts. **[8]**

 b Evaluate the usefulness of profit margin and liquidity ratio analysis to a retail business that operates several shops. **[12]**

30 Accounting fundamentals

Paper 2

Albion Builders (AB)

AB constructs new houses and apartments. The business accountant is worried about the profitability and liquidity of the business. He has managed to keep material costs as low as possible by buying cement and bricks in large quantities. However, advertising and head office expenses have increased. Operating profits are falling. Data taken from AB's latest income statement and statement of financial position are shown in Table 30.2.

AB has just completed three houses. It has taken longer than expected because of severe flooding three months ago. Two people are interested in the largest house. One person has offered a cash sale but for a price reduction of 10%. The other potential buyer does not want to move in for two months and will not pay before he moves. AB is still owed some money by the purchasers of one house who kept 5% back to make sure that AB corrected a window problem. Now this has been done, the owner has still not paid.

	2016	2017
Revenue ($m)	12	15
Cost of sales ($m)	8	10
Overhead expenses ($m)	2	3.5
Gross profit margin %	33.3	33.3
Operating profit margin %	16.7	See Q2a
Current ratio	1.2	1.0
Acid test ratio	0.6	0.3

Table 30.2 Summary of AB accounting data

1. **a** Define 'operating profit'. **[2]**
   b Briefly explain the term 'statement of financial position'. **[3]**
2. **a** Calculate the operating profit margin for 2017. **[3]**
   b Comment on the difference between the operating profit margin and the gross profit margin. **[3]**
3. Analyse **two** ways in which AB could improve its operating profit margin. **[8]**
4. Recommend to AB's managers how to improve the liquidity of the business. **[11]**

Improve this answer

This is a student's answer to Paper 1 Q3a.

Stakeholders will include workers and the lending bank. These groups will be interested in published accounts for the following reasons.

Workers will want to see if the product they are making is profitable and compare this profit with that made by other products the business makes. If the product they make is more profitable, then they will expect a pay rise and they will be confident that their jobs are secure.

Banks will want to know for sure whether the business will be able to pay them back the loans in the future. The liquidity ratios can be calculated and these will show the bank whether enough liquid assets will be available in a few years' time to pay back the total loan the company owes them.

Your challenge

This is a very weak answer! The student has misunderstood the information that published accounts contain. They do not provide information about each products' profitability. They do not indicate future liquidity – they are records of the past! A better answer is available on line – but write yours out first!

31 Forecasting and managing cash flows

Learning outcomes

The exercises in this chapter will help you to practise what you have learnt about:

- The need to hold a suitable level of cash within a business
- Understanding the construction of cash flow forecasts and their uses
- Recognising the uncertainty of cash flows
- Interpreting and amending simple cash flow forecasts from given data
- Methods of improving cash flows: debt factoring, sale and leaseback, leasing, hire purchase, reducing costs, managing trade receivables/payables
- Analysing situations in which the various methods of improving cash flow can be used.

KEY TERMS

Cash flow
Liquidation
Insolvent
Cash inflows
Cash outflows
Cash flow forecast
Net monthly cash flow

Opening cash balance
Closing cash balance
Credit control
Bad debt
Overtrading
Creditors (trade or accounts payable)

Key skills exercises

Knowledge and understanding

To answer the questions in this chapter, you need to know and understand:

- **how cash flows differ from profit earned**
- **net cash flows, cash inflows and cash outflows**
- **different ways to improve future cash flow position.**

1 What does the term 'net cash flow' mean?
2 State **two** reasons why the profit earned by a business in one month may not be the same as the net cash flow that month.
3 Why is cash more important than profit in the short run?
4 State **three** factors that can lead to cash flowing into a business.
5 State **three** factors that can result in cash outflows.
6 Differentiate between opening cash balance and closing cash balance.
7 State **two** possible causes of cash flow problems for a business.
8 State **two** ways a business could try to increase cash inflows.

9 State **two** ways a business could try to reduce cash outflows.

10 Outline **two** reasons why cash flow forecasts could be unreliable.

Knowledge, understanding and application

Remember to apply your answers to cash flow questions to the case study business as reasons for cash flow problems can depend on the type of business outlined in the case study.

Café Fajita (CF)

CF specialises in Mexican food such as fajitas and tacos. It has been open three weeks and already has a number of regular customers. Some pay cash and some pay with credit cards. It takes at least three weeks for CF to receive payment from the credit card operating companies. Local businesses have also started using CF to take clients for lunches. Business customers are offered four weeks' credit. The owners are two brothers with equal investments in the partnership. Ramos thinks his business is already making a profit but his brother, Antonio – who is responsible for accounts and administration – has just warned Ramos that the business is almost up to its overdraft limit. 'How can that be?' asked a surprised Ramos. 'We have doubled the number of customers since the first week.' Antonio sat Ramos down at the end of a busy day's trading and explained the following cash flow forecast to him.

Month	4	5	6	7	8	9
Cash in:						
Cash customers	4	4.2	4.4	4.6	5	5.4
Payments from credit card companies	0	1	1.2	1.3	1.5	1.7
Business accounts paid	2	2.1	2.3	2.5	2.7	3
Total cash in	6	7.3	7.9	8.4	9.2	Z
Cash out:						
Payments to food suppliers	2	3.1	3.3	3.8	4	4.5
Wage payments	2	2	2	2.2	2.4	2.4
Equipment leasing costs	1	1	1	1	1	1
Rent and other fixed costs	1	1	1	4	1	2
Advertising/promotions	2			1		2
Total cash out	(8)	(7.1)	(7.3)	(12)	(8.4)	(11.9)
Net cash flow	(2)	0.2	0.6	X	0.8	(1.8)
Opening balance	0.5	(1.5)	(1.3)	(0.7)	(4.3)	(3.5)
Closing balance	(1.5)	(1.3)	(0.7)	(4.3)	Y	(5.3)

Table 31.1 Cash flow forecast for CF: 4th to 9th week of trading ($000)

Ramos was amazed that CF was planning such a large overdraft. 'Have you included the big business lunch for AVA we are catering for in week 8?' asked Ramos. 'Yes of course', said Antonio. 'That should make us a good profit but it makes the cash flow worse, at least in that week. We have to pay "cash on delivery" to all of our suppliers as they do not give credit terms to start-up businesses like ours.'

11 Outline why cash flow forecasting is important for CF.

12 In week 8, why would you expect the profit made to be higher than the net cash flow?

13 Calculate values X, Y and Z.

14 Suggest **two** problems that CF might experience at the end of week 9.

15 Outline **two** reasons for the worrying trend in cash flow for CF.

16 Outline **two** ways in which monthly cash inflows could be increased.

17 Outline **two** ways in which monthly cash outflows could be reduced.

> **WORKED EXAMPLE**
>
> Advertising and promotion costs could be reduced, for example in week 9 it is planned to spend $2,000. **[K/Ap]** This seems unnecessary as CF already has a good customer base. **[Ap]**

Knowledge, understanding, application and analysis

Explaining the 'benefits and limitations' of cash flow forecasting and detailed explanations of ways to improve cash flow are examples of questions requiring the skill of analysis.

18 Analyse the limitations of the ways suggested to improve monthly cash inflows in answer to Q16.

19 Analyse limitations of the ways suggested to reduce monthly cash outflows suggested in answer to Q17.

> **WORKED EXAMPLE**
>
> By reducing advertising and promotion spending CF could see sales fall in future weeks. **[K]** We do not know how many of the regular customers are attracted by 'promotions' such as 'a free drink with a fajito'. **[Ap]** By cutting advertising and promotion spending so early in the life of the business could put at risk its future sales success. **[A]**

Knowledge, application, analysis and evaluation

The skill of evaluation requires that you make supported decisions, draw conclusions and prioritise factors.

20 Recommend the best ways for CF to avoid a cash flow crisis by week 9.

21 Evaluate the extent to which a reliable cash flow forecast will help to ensure CF's future success.

> **TIP**
> For Q21, explain the benefits of cash flow forecasting to CF making reference to Table 31.1. Explain the limitations of cash flow forecasting, for example it may be inaccurate. Consider other factors that will influence future success, such as how pleased the business customers is with the party for week 8. Come to an overall conclusion.

Exam-style questions

Paper 1

Section A

1. **a** Define 'cash flow forecast'. **(2)**

   b Explain **two** reasons why a cash flow forecast for a fashion clothing business might be inaccurate. **[5]**

Section B

2. **a** Analyse how a profitable business can have cash flow problems. **[8]**

   b Evaluate the usefulness of cash flow forecasts to a new business start-up in social media. **[12]**

Paper 2

> **Henri's Computer Repairs (HCR)**
>
> Henri set up his business three years ago. He repairs all types of computers and tablets. He is surprised by how many business customers he has. HCR gives these customers three months to pay bills. When he started, Henri expected mainly private customers who would pay in cash for repairs to home computers. He employs five skilled computer engineers who are always very busy. He can trust them to fix any problem quickly and efficiently. He pays them high wages and a monthly bonus for completing repairs before the estimated time. HCR has other costs too. Each engineer needs a van and specialist testing equipment. Several of the vehicles and some of the test equipment need replacing and Henri plans to buy these in two to three months' time. HCR started operating from Henri's garage but it now rents a new building on an industrial estate. This, Henri thinks, helps to promote the business. HCR also promotes itself via its website and an advertisement in a local business newspaper.
>
> HCR's accountant has asked Henri to look at the latest cash flow forecast. The accountant suggested that urgent action – such as use of debt factoring – is needed to prevent an overdraft becoming necessary. Henri suggested raising prices to cash customers by 20% in month 3 and reducing promotion by 50% in that month as two ways of improving the cash flow position.

31 Forecasting and managing cash flows

An extract of the cash flow forecast is shown in Table 31.2.

	Month 1	Month 2	Month 3
Cash in:			
Cash sales	5	5	6
Business accounts paid	12	13	15
Total cash in	17	18	21
Cash out:			
Rent	3	3	3
Wages and bonuses	8	10	9
Computer spare parts	2	3	4
Promotion and other costs	1	1	3
Capital expenditure	0	15	6
Total cash out	14	32	Z
Net cash flow	3	Y	(4)
Opening balance	X	11	(3)
Closing balance	11	(3)	(7)

Table 31.2 Extract from HCR's cash flow forecast – next three months ($000)

1 a Define 'debt factoring'. **[2]**

   b Briefly explain the term 'net cash flow'. **[3]**

2 a Calculate the values of X, Y and Z. **[3]**

   b Outline **one** problem for HCR if it reaches the end of month 3 with the closing balance indicated. **[3]**

3 Analyse the likely impact on HCR's cash flow position by the end of month 3 if the changes suggested by Henri are made. State any assumptions made. **[8]**

4 Recommend which is the best way for HCR to improve its cash flow position. **[11]**

Improve this answer

This is a student's answer to Paper 1 Q2a. Skills are shown in brackets to help you.

> Profit is revenue less costs. Net cash flow is cash in minus cash out. [K] In a business where all payments and revenue are in cash, profit and cash flow could be the same. In most businesses there will be some credit. Credit can be offered by suppliers where supplies arrive but do not have to be paid for immediately. Credit can be offered to customers where products are delivered but the customer is given time to pay. So a profit or loss might be made but the cash received will be different. [An]

Your challenge

This answer starts well and there is evidence of good understanding. However, only one example is used and this is not well explained in sufficient analytical detail. It is not clear why cash flow will be different from profit – and it does not refer to cash flow problems either. See whether you can improve this answer. A better one is available on line – but write yours out first!

32 Costs (A Level only)

Learning outcomes

The exercises in this chapter will help you to practise what you have learnt about:

- The difference between full costing and contribution costing; contribution and profit
- The uses and limitations of both costing methods
- Assessing when these methods could be used
- Solving numerical problems involving full costing and contribution costing data
- Applying contribution costing to 'accept/reject' order decisions.

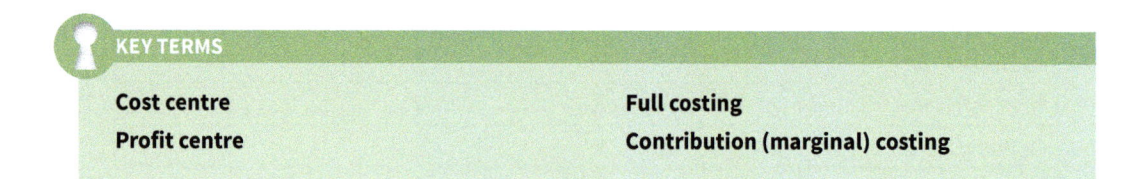

KEY TERMS

Cost centre	Full costing
Profit centre	Contribution (marginal) costing

Key skills exercises

Knowledge and understanding

To answer the questions in this chapter, you need to know and understand:

- **what full costing means**
- **what contribution costing means**
- **the problems of accurately allocating fixed/overhead costs.**

1. Differentiate between a 'cost centre' and a 'profit centre'.
2. State **one** reason why it is difficult to allocate overheads to products or cost centres.
3. Why would a business making and selling just one type of product have no problems in 'allocating overheads'?
4. State **one** possible advantage of full costing.
5. What is meant by the term 'contribution cost'?
6. How can selling a product for less than its 'full cost' add to the profit of a business?
7. Why might a business not decide to outsource production of a component even though it is being offered for a price less than the full cost of making it within the business?
8. Why might a business decide to continue to make a product which makes a 'loss' when using full costing?

32 Costs (A Level only)

Knowledge, understanding and application

Remember to apply your answers to the case study business. Read the case study thoroughly and use the information it contains to support your answers.

> ### Café Fajita (CF) (see also Chapter 31)
>
> The catering for the AVA company in week 8 was so successful that the AVA's manager has asked for the same food and drink to be provided for 40 clients. This event would take place twice a month. The manager is prepared to pay $25 per person. Ramos and Antonio looked at the costs involved before deciding whether to accept this contract. They collected the information in Table 32.1.
>
> | | |
> |---|---|
> | Variable cost (food and drink) per client | $12 |
> | Variable cost – labour cost of each AVA event | $360 |
> | Allocated café overhead costs to each AVA event (Antonio's estimate) | $240 |
>
> **Table 32.1** CF cost data for AVA business catering
>
> 'It would be madness to accept this contract', said Ramos. 'We are going to make a loss each time and we are already busy in the café. Suppose we have to pay overtime rates to our employees if we are too busy in the café?'
>
> 'Wait', said Antonio, 'AVA is a really big company with many clients. My allocation of overheads was an estimate based on the proportion of our total variable costs the contract will account for. I think we could actually increase CF's profit if we accepted this contract.'

9 Identify **two** overhead costs of the business.

10 Outline why these overhead costs are difficult to allocate or apportion to the new business contract.

11 Calculate the full cost of each AVA event using the allocation figure suggested by Ramos.

> ### WORKED EXAMPLE
>
> Full cost = Variable + Allocated overheads
> = [($12 × 40) + $360] + $240 = $1,080
>
> Unit full cost = $27 per client [$1,080/40]

12 Calculate the profit or loss on each AVA event.

13 Calculate the contribution made by each AVA event.

14 Apart from the revenue/cost data, suggest **two** qualitative factors that Ramos and Antonio should consider before accepting or rejecting this contract.

Knowledge, understanding, application and analysis

Explaining the 'benefits and limitations' of accepting a new contract using both cost and revenue data and qualitative information is usually the most common form of analysis expected in this syllabus area.

15 Analyse **two** likely limitations of Antonio's attempt to allocate overhead costs.

16 Analyse the impact on CF's profit if the business accepts the contract to supply catering for two AVA events each month.

> **WORKED EXAMPLE**
>
> For this type of decision we ignore overhead costs. As they are indirect they will not have been incurred as a result of accepting this contract and they will not increase if the contract is accepted. **[K]** Contribution costing is therefore used. If the contract makes a positive contribution to overheads and profit, then the total profit of the business will increase. **[A]**
>
> The contribution from accepting this contract will be:
>
> = Total revenue − Total Variable costs
>
> = [40 × $25] − [($12 × 40) + $360]
>
> = $1,000 − $840
>
> = $160 per event
>
> 24 events per year (2 per month) so total contribution = 24 × $160 = $3,840 **[Ap]**
>
> If there are no other direct costs incurred as a result of this contract (special equipment or overtime for employees?) then CF's annual profit will increase by $3,840 from accepting the contract. **[A]**

Knowledge, application, analysis and evaluation

The skill of evaluation requires that you make supported decisions, draw conclusions and give recommendations.

17 Recommend whether CF should accept this contract from AVA. Justify your answer by using your quantitative results to previous questions and qualitative information.

> **TIP**
> Will the contract increase or reduce CF's profit? What other factors should be considered before the brothers make this decision?

32 Costs (A Level only)

Exam-style questions

Paper 3

Special TVs (STV)

STV make some of the largest televisions on the market. The business has a reputation for excellent quality products and innovative design and engineering. The STV brand and associated logo are well recognised in customer research. The business currently operates at 80% of capacity. STV is profitable but the newly appointed CEO wants to drive down costs but maintain quality. She aims to use retained earnings to finance additional research and development to keep STV as brand leader.

She has identified the TV speaker department as a potential area of the factory's output that could be outsourced to save on costs. The space created could be used for the CEO's proposed new home cinema screen project. The CEO has obtained an offer from a foreign company with electronics experience to supply STV with TV speakers of the same specification as those made in-house. The cost per speaker would be $34. She wants to compare this with the cost of STV produced speakers – see Table 32.2.

	STV speaker production
Direct labour cost per unit	$14
Direct material cost per unit	$18
Overhead cost per unit – based on output level of 800 speakers per month	$12

Table 32.2 STV speaker production costs

STV's Marketing Director has been asked by HiQRetail plc to supply 200 STV products each month. HiQRetail wants the TV frame to be redesigned slightly and the products rebranded with its own name and logo. It is trying to become better known as an own-brand retailer of quality electronic products. The retail company has offered to pay $900 per TV. In discussion with HiQRetail, STV's Marketing Director discovered that the retailer was also in negotiation with another manufacturer of large TVs. The Marketing Director promised to give HiQRetail a reply within one week after the possible contract had been discussed at the next Board meeting. Table 32.3 shows the data that the Marketing Director wanted discussed at that meeting.

Direct labour cost per unit	$320
Direct material cost per unit	$240
Unit cost of making design changes	$25
Overhead cost per unit – based on current output level of 800 TV's per month	$400

Table 32.3 Cost of producing TV's for HiQRetail

Cambridge AS and A Level Business

1. **a** Calculate the impact on STV's profit if it accepts the outsourcing offer, stating the assumptions made. **[8]**

   b Recommend to the directors whether the outsourcing offer should be accepted. Use your result to 1a and other information to justify your answer. **[12]**

2. **a** Calculate the impact on STV's profit if it accepts the offer from the retailer. **[6]**

   b Recommend to the directors whether the contract with the retailer should be accepted. Use your result to 2a and other information to justify your answer. **[12]**

Improve this answer

This is a student's answer to Q1a. Skills are shown in brackets to help you.

Outsourcing TV speakers to the foreign supplier seems to be cheaper – $34 per unit rather than the full cost of making in STV factory of $44 [K/Ap]. However, the overhead costs allocated to the speaker division will still have to be paid – they are fixed costs [Ap/An]. They should therefore be ignored when considering the impact on profit of this offer. So the direct cost of STV making speakers is only $32 per unit which is $2 less than the offer by the foreign supplier [Ap/An]. So, the impact on costs of accepting this outsourcing offer will be an additional direct cost of $2 per unit – or $1600 per month. Profit will be reduced by this amount if the outsourcing offer is accepted [An].

I have assumed that the allocation of overhead costs is accurate and that these costs e.g. factory overheads, cannot be quickly allocated to another product e.g. the new proposed home cinema screen division [Ap].

Your challenge

This answer is accurate and contains some well-argued assumptions. Your challenge is to use this information to write an answer to Q1b. An example answer is given online – but write yours out first!

33 Budgets (A Level only)

Learning outcomes

The exercises in this chapter will help you to practise what you have learnt about:

- What budgets are and why measuring performance is important
- The benefits and drawbacks of budgets/budgeting: allocating resources, controlling and monitoring of a business
- The role of budgets in appraising business
- The meaning of variances
- Calculating and interpreting variances.

KEY TERMS

Budget
Budget holder
Variance analysis
Delegated budgets
Incremental budgeting

Zero budgeting
Flexible budgeting
Adverse variance
Favourable variance

Key skills exercises

Knowledge and understanding

To answer the questions in this chapter, you need to know and understand:
- **what budgets are and how budgeting aids business control and monitoring**
- **different ways in which budgets can be set**
- **how budgets and actual performance are compared using variance analysis.**

1 Differentiate between a budget and a forecast.
2 Give **one** reason why a new start-up business should set budgets.
3 Why might there be a benefit in asking the budget holder to be involved in setting budgets?
4 State **one** problem that might result from all departments being able to set their own budgets independently of each other.
5 How do budgets allocate resources?
6 How can budgets help to control and monitor a business?
7 Differentiate between zero budgets and flexible budgets.
8 Does an adverse variance mean that profit is higher or lower than budgeted?
9 State **one** possible cause of a favourable variable cost variance.
10 State **one** possible cause of an adverse fixed cost variance.
11 State **one** possible reason for a favourable revenue variance.

Knowledge, understanding and application

Remember to apply your answers to the business context of the case study.

Greybridge College (GC)

GC offers a range of courses to students from the age of 16. Many of its students are adults who want the chance to further their education. GC is organised into subject departments. Each department is given an annual budget containing details of the expected revenue, direct costs and allocated overheads for the next 12 months. The Principal of GC sets these budgets based mainly on the performance of each department over the previous year. Some adjustment is made for inflation and for changes in the popularity of certain subjects. Heads of Department are expected to meet these budget targets and are held to account if they do not.

Some departments have set higher prices for their courses than others. Those that have to work with small groups, require a lot of equipment or expensive materials are expected to charge more than those subjects that are largely classroom based with the potential to teach large classes. The budget for the Science department for the 12 months just ended is shown in Table 33.1. The actual outcomes are also shown.

	Budget	Actual
Revenue	528	505
Direct labour cost	335	346
Direct material cost	73	70
Allocated overheads	45	48

Table 33.1 Science department budget and actual outcomes – last 12 months ($000)

12 Calculate the variances for the last 12 months.

13 Indicate whether the variances are favourable or adverse.

WORKED EXAMPLE

The revenue variance is ($23,000), which is adverse as it has the effect of reducing the contribution/profits made by this department. **[K/Ap]**

14 Suggest **one** reason for the revenue variance.

15 Suggest **one** reason for the direct materials variance.

16 Suggest **one** reason for the labour direct cost variance.

17 Outline **two** benefits to GC of setting budgets.

18 Does GC appear to use incremental budgeting or zero budgeting? Explain your answer.

33 Budgets (A Level only)

Knowledge, understanding, application and analysis

Explaining the benefits and limitations of budgeting and analysing the different approaches to budgeting are important examples of 'analyse' questions. Analysing the causes of variances and the usefulness of variance analysis will also be examined.

19 Analyse the limitations of budgeting process at GC.

20 Analyse **one** benefit to GC of using zero budgeting.

> **WORKED EXAMPLE**
>
> Zero budgeting means 'starting from zero' and the explaining or justifying the budgets for the next future time period. **[K]** This could help GC as last year's budget might not be a good basis for setting budgets for the next year. If a new Technology department has opened within GC, then this could take students away from Science so it would be misleading to just base budgets on last year's figures. **[Ap]** It would be more accurate to assess, from the new situation, what the demand for and needs of the Science department are now likely to be. Its performance could be monitored more accurately. **[A]**

21 Analyse **one** benefit to GC of using delegated budgeting.

> **TIP**
>
> For Q23, assess the problems with the current GC budgeting system, and analyse how changes might improve it (e.g. consider zero or flexible budgets and Head of Department involvement in setting budgets). Finally, make clear recommendations.

Knowledge, application, analysis and evaluation

The skill of evaluation requires that you make supported decisions, draw conclusions and prioritise factors.

22 Recommend action that GC could take to reduce the chances of adverse variances in future.

23 Discuss the improvements GC could take to improve the budgeting process.

Exam-style questions

Paper 3

Best Supermarket (BS)

BS operates a large out-of-town supermarket. It sells fresh and frozen food, drinks, children's clothes and kitchen tools. It is owned and managed by the Best family. The current Managing Director, Ros, is proud of her employees. Most have been with the business for many years and they like Ros's laissez-faire leadership style, which gives them a lot of freedom and responsibility.

Despite the good employer–employee relationship, last year Ros had major concerns about BS. Revenue and profits fell for each of the last three years. 'I can tell from the accounts that we are not doing as well as a few years ago but they do not tell me why or which departments are producing disappointing results,' she told family members.

'I think we need a clearer set of targets for each department,' said Joe, her son who had just taken Business A Level. 'But I don't set targets,' said Ros, 'as I assume that the employees know we are trying to sell more each year.'

Joe suggested setting clear budgets for each of the departments of the shop. 'You could treat them like mini businesses with their own revenue, cost and profit targets,' he said.

That was last year. Since then Ros and Joe have worked together to give each department monthly budgets. These are compared with actual results and discussed each month with the manager of each department. An example for the frozen food department is shown in Table 33.2:

	Budget	Actual
Revenue	13	10
Direct labour cost	5	6
Direct material cost	3	2
Allocated overheads	2	2
Monthly profit	3	0

Table 33.2 Budget and actual data for frozen food department – last month ($000)

When these data were discussed, the manager of the department was surprised that Ros and Joe had not taken several factors into account. 'When you set the budget for last month, didn't you know that we had a planned maintenance programme for the freezers which meant shutting some of them down for a week? This reduced the number of items that were available on display. The labour cost was higher because of the maintenance costs. One new range of frozen ready meals sold very well last month but this did not show up in your budget because there is just one figure for the whole department. I think you just take the previous month's figures and 'add a bit on' which I don't think is the right way to budget for this business.'

1 Analyse the benefits to BS of setting monthly departmental budgets. **[10]**
2 Evaluate how budgeting within BS could be made more effective. **[14]**

Annotate this answer

This is a student's answer to Q2.

BS now has a system of budgeting which is better than not having budgets at all. However, several improvements could be made to ensure the budgets are even more effective at measuring and monitoring performance. Ros and Joe do not seem to involve the departmental managers when setting budgets. They seem to decide on the budgets and just hand them out to each department as targets to be met. Having targets can be beneficial as it gives a clear focus to each department to work towards. However, if it is thought that targets are very difficult or impossible to achieve then they just demotivate. This seems to be the case at BS. According to the frozen food department manager, it was going to be impossible to meet the revenue target for last month because of the planned maintenance programme for the freezers. If the manager had been consulted and had participated in the budget setting then the targets set could have been more realistic and more motivating.

Similarly, if Ros and Joe had bothered to ask, they would have found out that labour costs were going to be higher last month due to maintenance costs for the freezers, which are clearly a direct cost as they do not apply to any other department. It seems unreasonable to criticise the frozen food manager and his department for not meeting a profit target when two factors could have been discussed with Joe and Ros before the budget was set.

33 Budgets (A Level only)

Perhaps the most important change that should be made with the BS budgeting system is to encourage participation with managers in setting these monthly targets. The managers and their departments will then be much more motivated in trying to achieve them as well as the involvement leading to much more realistic budgets to start with.

Other changes that would make budgeting at BS more effective would be to break them down into smaller units. For example, having one big budget for frozen food is less helpful than having budgets for each major range of frozen foods – such as meat, pizzas, vegetables and so on. This would allow much more accurate monitoring of the sales performance of each type of frozen food and corrective action could be directed to that range of food that was underperforming. This would save managers' time by directing their attention to the range of products that are under-performing.

The other main change that should be made is the use of zero budgeting for some products rather than 'take last month's figure and add some on' as the frozen food manager seems to be suggesting. This means that the existing budgets will not take into account new ranges being introduced in the shop – which should increase sales. It also means that the monthly budgets ignore seasonal effects and more frozen food might be bought by consumers in the winter as fewer fresh products are available. Again, participation by each departmental manager in the setting of budgets would have allowed these seasonal variations to be reflected in the budgets – which suggests that involvement and participation in the setting of budgets is the key improvement that BS should make. This change should be easy to make at BS because the employees seem loyal and are well respected by senior managers so the introduction of participation should be easy to achieve.

Your challenge

This is a good answer that displays very good understanding of budgets. The points made are well explained and analysed. Do you agree that the answer is well applied to BS? Can you identify the key evaluative points? Annotate this answer with the skills. An annotated version of the answer is available online – but mark this copy first!

(A Level only)

Learning outcomes

The exercises in this chapter will help you to practise what you have learnt about:

- Making simple amendments to Statements of financial position and income statements and understanding the relationships between these two statements
- The importance of accounting for the depreciation of fixed assets and calculate depreciation using the straight-line method
- The impact of depreciation on the final accounts of a business
- The impact on the published accounts of changes in the value of inventories and non-current assets; inventories, goodwill, and net realisable value.

KEY TERMS

Intellectual property	Depreciation
Market value	Net book value
Capital expenditure	Straight-line depreciation
Revenue expenditure	Net realisable value

Key skills exercises

Knowledge and understanding

To answer the questions in this chapter, you need to know and understand:

- **what depreciation is, why it occurs and how to account for it**
- **the straight-line depreciation formula**
- **how goodwill arises**
- **what net realisable value means and how to account for it.**

1. State **two** reasons why many non-current assets depreciate in value.
2. State the formula for straight-line depreciation.
3. Other things remaining unchanged, what happens to annual depreciation if the expected useful life of a non-current asset is reduced?
4. What happens to the profit of a business when depreciation is included in the accounts?
5. How does depreciation affect the net asset value of non-current assets?
6. Why would profit be recorded inaccurately if depreciation was not applied to a non-current asset but the cost of it was recorded i) when it was first bought; ii) when it was disposed of?
7. How does a lower valuation of inventories which have been held for over a year affect the published accounts of a business?
8. How is goodwill treated on published accounts?

9 What is meant by 'net realisable value'?

10 Why are inventories not recorded on published accounts at their expected selling price?

Knowledge, understanding and application

Remember to apply the straight-line depreciation formula accurately, selecting the appropriate data from the case study.

Hurtwood Computing (HC)

HC is a limited company that retails computer hardware and software. It operates two large retail shops. Its latest income statement is almost ready to be published and is summarised in Table 34.1.

	$000
Revenue	1,500
Cost of sales	800
Gross profit	X
Expenses (inc. depreciation)	400
Operating profit	Y
Tax (@40%)	120
Profit for the year	180
Dividends	Z
Retained earnings	100

Table 34.1 Summary of HC's latest income statement

Several days before the accounts were published, an accountant in the finance department identified two pieces of information that had not been included in the income statement. There is still time to make amendments before the accounts are published.

Firstly, a new truck had been purchased at the start of the financial year. The cost of this had not been recorded on the accounts. HC depreciates vehicles over an estimated useful life of four years. The truck is expected to be worth 20% of its purchase price in five years' time. It cost HC $40,000.

Secondly, one brand of tablet computer has sold less well than expected; 500 units of this tablet remain in inventory even though they were purchased by HC over six months ago. They were bought for $120 each but have been replaced by more advanced models. HC was planning to retail them for $160 each but the Marketing Director thinks they might have to be sold at a 75% discount on this price. 'No one wants last year's model of tablet,' he explained to HC's CEO.

11 Calculate the missing values, X, Y and Z.

12 Calculate the annual depreciation of the new truck.

Cambridge AS and A Level Business

> **WORKED EXAMPLE**
>
> New truck: Straight-line annual depreciation $= \dfrac{\text{Purchase price} - \text{Residual value}}{\text{Length of useful life}}$
>
> $= \dfrac{\$40,000 - 8,000}{4}$
>
> $= \$8,000$

13 Amend the income statement showing the annual depreciation of this truck.

14 Comment on the differences between this income statement and the original one shown in Table 34.1.

15 Recalculate the cost of sales based on the new net realisable value for the inventory of the tablet computers held for more than six months.

16 Amend the income statement in Table 34.1 showing both the depreciation amendment and the net realisable value amendment.

Knowledge, understanding, application and analysis

Explaining the impact of changes in the valuation of assets on the statement of financial position is an important analytical skill demanded by questions based on this chapter.

17 Analyse **two** benefits to HC of accurate recording of depreciation.

18 Analyse the benefit to HC of accurate recording of net realisable values (NRV) for inventories.

> **WORKED EXAMPLE**
>
> If the original purchase price of these tablet computers had been used on HC's published accounts then this would have been higher than the NRV **[K]** by $80 per unit. **[Ap]** This would have led to the cost of sales being too low and annual recorded profit too high. **[A]** This higher profit figure could mislead stakeholders into believing the business is performing better that it actually is and could lead to the share price being overvalued. Once the tablets are sold, a loss would have to be recorded on them, 'surprising' stakeholders and possibly resulting in a lower share price. **[A]**

Knowledge, application, analysis and evaluation

The skill of evaluation requires that you make supported decisions, draw conclusions and prioritise factors.

19 Discuss the view that the valuation of HC's assets can never be entirely accurate so the published accounts should not be relied upon by stakeholders.

> **TIP**
>
> Explain how current and non-current assets should be recorded. Analyse the problems of accurate valuation. Evaluate whether stakeholders can rely on published accounts based on these points.

34 Contents of published accounts (A Level only)

Exam-style questions

Paper 3

Park Bay Printers (PBP)

PBP is a public limited company. It is one of the largest newspaper and book printers in the country. It is a successful business and two attempts have been made to take it over in recent years. These failed because the shareholders have trust in the directors to deliver high dividends each year and they also benefit from a rising share price. PBP is based in a large city centre site that it purchased 30 years ago. It uses a special colour printing process that PBP patented several years ago.

PBP has just purchased a large digitally controlled printing press that will save on labour costs. The purchase price of the press was $5 million. The machine it replaces lasted for 25 years but the CEO of PBP has explained to the directors that 'with the rapid pace of technological change, we cannot expect this new press to still be economically viable after about five years. It could be worth only $0.5m at the end of its economically useful life.'

The owners of a rival printing business, HZP, are studying PBP's latest accounts. A summary from the statement of financial position is shown in Table 34.2. HZP's main shareholder said: 'I think this business is undervaluing its non-current assets. If we put in a takeover bid for its shares above their current price, I believe we could still be buying up the company cheaply as it has so much goodwill.'

	$m
Property	12
Equipment and vehicles	23
Intangible assets	1
Total assets	39
Retained earnings	30
Total equity and liabilities	39

Table 34.2 Summary of PBP's latest statement of financial position

1. **a** Calculate annual depreciation for the new printing press. **[2]**

   b Analyse **two** reasons why this annual amount might not, in fact, be accurate. **[8]**

2. Assess the importance to PBP of measuring the value of its non-current and current assets as accurately as possible. **[14]**

Improve this answer

This is a student's answer to Q2. Skills are shown in brackets to help you.

Non-current assets are those that are expected to be owned and used for more than one year. They include property, machinery and vehicles. [K] Current assets include trade receivables and inventories. The valuation of most of these assets can never be entirely accurate. How much is a plot of land or a building worth? The only way to find out is to sell these assets, which most businesses do not want to do. Therefore, estimates have to be made each year when the accounts are published. With PBP's site, bought 30 years ago, it would be really misleading if the original purchase price was still being used on the accounts. [Ap] The value has probably appreciated greatly – but by how much? Any estimate used on PBP's accounts might be inaccurate and H2P might have some property experts who believe that the site is worth more than PBP's accounts actually state.

Equipment and machinery depreciates. As the CEO said, with the pace of change, depreciation is now more difficult to predict. If assets such as a printing machine go out of date more quickly than expected, it might have to be replaced 'early' and this means that the annual depreciation and net book value have been calculated inaccurately. [An]

Intangible assets are difficult to value. PBP has a patent on a printing process and it is not clear how this has been valued. [Ap] If it would cost a rival business more than $1m to develop a similar process, then PBP has probably undervalued its intangible assets.

Current assets are also difficult to value accurately especially debts which might turn out to be 'bad' and inventories. PBP might have some paper inventory which has been damaged in a water leak – how should this paper now be recorded on PBP's accounts? It would be misleading, perhaps, to record it as being valued at its original purchase prices. [An]

The valuation of all of these assets obviously affects the total value of the business.

Your challenge

This answer shows evidence of good understanding and there is some good application to the case study business. However, the consequences of inaccurate valuations of assets are not analysed in any detail and there is very limited evaluation. A better answer is available online – but write yours out first!

(A Level only)

Learning outcomes

The exercises in this chapter will help you to practise what you have learnt about:

- Calculating and analysing the meaning of return on capital employed; inventory turnover; days' sales in receivables
- Calculating and analysing the meaning of gearing
- Calculating and analysing the meaning of the investor ratios: dividend yield, dividend cover, price/earnings ratio
- How each of the ratios is used
- Analysing reasons for the results obtained
- Strategies that businesses might adopt to improve ratio results
- Analysing comparisons of ratio results between businesses
- The limitations of the accounting ratios.

KEY TERMS

Return on capital employed (RoCE)
Capital employed
Inventory turnover ratio
Day's sales in receivables ratio
Share price
Dividend

Dividend yield ratio
Dividend per share
Dividend cover ratio
Price/earnings ratio
Earnings per share

Key skills exercises

Knowledge and understanding

To answer the questions in this chapter, you need to know and understand:

- **all of the ratios listed in Key Terms and how to calculate the data needed for them (e.g. earnings per share)**
- **how ratio analysis can be used**
- **how businesses can improve ratio results.**

1. State **two** reasons why a business records a lower return on capital employed (RoCE) this year than last year.
2. Why is a high inventory turnover ratio an indication of an efficient business?
3. Why is it unreasonable to compare the inventory turnover ratios of two businesses in very different industries?
4. What would a policy of using debt factors do to the day's sales in receivables ratio?
5. State **two** reasons why the dividend yield ratio could increase.
6. What does a high dividend cover ratio indicate about the strategy of the management of that business?

7   State the price earnings ratio formula.

8   State **two** reasons for a price earnings ratio increase between two years.

9   State **one** way in which the inventory turnover ratio could be increased.

10 State **one** way in which the gearing ratio could be reduced.

Knowledge, understanding and application

Remember to apply the correct ratio formula to the question asked and to identify the appropriate data required for the formula from the case study.

Sports Gear (SG)

SG manufactures fashionable sports shoes. They are bought not just by consumers who want quality shoes for playing sports such as tennis and golf but also by consumers who want them as fashion accessories to match their designer clothes. SG sells only to exclusive sports or fashion retailers and it does not allow online purchases to be made. SG's Finance Director is analysing the company's accounts using key ratios. She thinks that SG's financial performance is being badly affected by several factors:

- increasing interest rates, which are reducing consumers' discretionary incomes
- the failure of the latest design of sports shoe to reach sales targets – production levels have not yet been cut to reflect these disappointing sales
- demands from retailers for longer credit periods.

The Finance Director started to calculate the important ratios. As she did so, she wondered whether it had been a good idea for SG to increase borrowing in 2017 to finance the purchase of land to build an extension to its main factory. This building work had not yet started. Her thoughts also turned to how to improve the results for next year and whether a reduction in the rates of depreciation on non-current assets would be noticed by stakeholders.

	2016	2017
Capital employed (as at 31/12/17) ($m)	35	38
Operating profit (for year) ($m)	7	6
Cost of sales (for year) ($m)	19	20
Inventories (as at 31/12/17) ($m)	1	2
Non-current liabilities (as at 31/12/17) ($m)	16	19
Revenue (for year) ($m)	40	42
Trade accounts receivable (as at 31/12/17) ($m)	3	4
Dividend per share ($)	2	2
Share price (31/12/17) ($)	15	12
Earnings per share ($)	4	3

Table 35.1 Selected financial data for SG

11 Calculate the RoCE in 2016.

35 Analysis of published accounts (A Level only)

> **WORKED EXAMPLE**
>
> RoCE % = $\dfrac{\text{Operating profit}}{\text{Capital employed}} \times 100$
>
> $= \dfrac{7}{35} \times 100$
>
> $= 20\%$

12 Calculate the RoCE in 2017.

13 Comment on the likely causes of the different results to Q11 and Q12.

14 Calculate the gearing ratio for 2016 (Long-term loans/Capital employed × 100).

15 Calculate the gearing ratio for 2017.

16 Comment on your results to Q14 and Q15.

17 Calculate the inventory turnover for both years.

18 Comment on the likely causes of the different results of your answers to Q17.

19 Calculate the days sales in receivables ratio for both years.

20 Comment on the likely causes of the different results to Q19.

21 Calculate the dividend yield ratio for both years.

22 Comment on your results to Q21.

23 Calculate the price earnings ratio for both years.

24 Comment on your results to Q23.

Knowledge, understanding, application and analysis

Explaining the causes of changes in ratio results and how these results might be improved in future are important ways in which skills of analysis will be tested in this chapter.

25 Analyse **one** reason for the change in the price earnings ratio.

26 Analyse **one** problem that SG might experience as a consequence of the increased gearing ratio.

27 Analyse **two** ways in which SG could attempt to increase its inventory turnover ratio.

28 Analyse **two** ways in which SG could attempt to improve its RoCE ratio.

> **WORKED EXAMPLE**
>
> One way in which RoCE could be improved would be to sell off under-performing assets or assets no longer required by SG and use the finance raised to pay back some loans. **[K]** This would reduce the capital employed in the business and if operating profit was not affected, the RoCE would increase. **[A]** Although the land for the factory extension has only just been purchased, sales of the latest shoe design are disappointing so additional factory space might not be required so the land could be resold. **[Ap]**

Cambridge AS and A Level Business

Knowledge, application, analysis and evaluation

The skill of evaluation requires that you make supported decisions, draw conclusions and give recommendations.

29 Discuss the most important decisions that SG's directors should make to improve the company's accounting ratio results.

30 Discuss how the ratio analysis you have undertaken on SG's accounts could be made more useful to its shareholders and **one** other stakeholder group.

> **TIP**
>
> For Q30, consider what the two stakeholder groups are looking for in accounts. Would more years' results be useful. Comparison with other companies could be considered – but which ones? Would other ratios be useful too? Are the accounts 'window dressed'? The Finance Director seems to be considering this for next year. You will need to give an overall conclusion.

Exam-style questions

Paper 3

Acme Builders Limited (ABL)

ABL constructs apartments and houses. The company buys sites suitable for development and constructs new properties for sale to families who will live in them or to investors who will rent them out. The Finance Director has just completed the following ratio analysis shown in Table 35.2.

Return on capital employed	9% (12%)
Gearing ratio (Long-term loans/Capital employed × 100)	55% (45%)
Inventory turnover	2 (2.5)
Days sales in trade receivables	35 (23)
Dividend yield	4% (3%)
Price earnings ratio	8 (6)

Table 35.2 Selected accounting ratios for ABL – current year (previous year)

He also intends to calculate the dividend cover ratio (3 last year). He knows that total dividends this year were $5 million ($4 million last year), there were 50 million shares issued and the profit for the year was $10 million.

He is worried about the impact of the economic recession on the demand for the large apartments and houses that ABL specialises in. The decision to increase long-term loans this year was taken before the recession occurred. This external finance was used to increase the number of building sites that ABL holds in its land inventory. Other inventories include the most common building materials that ABL uses on all of its building sites.

35 Analysis of published accounts (A Level only)

1 a Calculate the dividend cover ratio for this year. **[4]**

  b Using your results to 1a and the data in Table 35.2, comment on whether the shareholders should be satisfied with the performance of ABL. **[12]**

2 Discuss the most effective ways for ABL to improve the RoCE ratio and the inventory turnover in future. **[14]**

Improve this answer

This is a student's answer to Q1b. Skills are shown in brackets to help you.

Shareholders might have mixed feelings about the performance of ABL but, generally, they will be disappointed. [E – if supported by later analysis] Dividend payments were higher this year than last [Ap] and shareholders want high dividends – as long as this does not reduce the company's ability to invest and expand for the future. [A] High dividends can reduce retained earnings – an important source of internal finance. It could be that ABL are trying to 'keep shareholders quiet' by increasing dividends even though other aspects of the company's performance is much weaker than last year. [A] A higher PE ratio is usually a good sign for shareholders but not if it is caused by a lower earnings per share figure. [A]

Shareholders also want high share prices. We are not told what the share price is and this is essential information before a final assessment of shareholder satisfaction can be made. [E] They will not be pleased about the lower RoCE or the higher gearing and lower inventory turnover.

So, on balance, the shareholders are unlikely to be satisfied with ABL's performance. [E – weak overall]

Your challenge

This answer has some strengths – but it could have been so much better. None of the actual results are referred to. There is no attempt to refer to the nature of the industry ABL is in or the state of the economy. The inadequacy of the data provided is hinted at – but more detail could have been given. The 'meaning' of the investor ratios is not explained. A better answer is available online – but write yours out first!

36 Investment appraisal (A Level only)

Learning outcomes

The exercises in this chapter will help you to practise what you have learnt about:

- The importance of appraising investment projects and the information needed to do this
- Why forecasting future cash flows from a project is a cause of uncertainty
- Calculating the payback period and evaluating its usefulness
- Calculating the average rate of return and evaluating its usefulness
- Calculating net present value and discounted payback and evaluating their usefulness
- Understanding the internal rate of return and evaluate its usefulness
- The importance of qualitative and quantitative factors in investment decisions.

KEY TERMS

Investment appraisal
Annual forecasted net cash flow
Payback period
Accounting rate of return (ARR)
Net present value (NPV)
Internal rate of return (IRR)
Criterion rates or levels

Key skills exercises

Knowledge and understanding

To answer the questions in this chapter, you need to know and understand:
- the relevant formulae and methods of calculating investment appraisal
- drawbacks to each of these methods
- common qualitative factors used in investment appraisal.

1. What is meant by 'the payback on this project is three years'?
2. Why is a quick payback often preferred by businesses?
3. State **one** limitation of the payback method of investment appraisal.
4. What is meant by 'the ARR for this project is 13%'?
5. Why is a high ARR preferable to a low one?
6. State **one** limitation of the ARR method of investment appraisal.
7. What is meant by 'discounted cash flow'?
8. What is meant by 'the net present value of this project is $3.6 million'?
9. What would happen to this net present value (NPV) if the discount rate was raised?
10. State one limitation of the NPV method of investment appraisal.
11. What is meant by 'the discounted payback on this project is two years'?

36 Investment appraisal (A Level only)

12 What would happen to this time period if the discount factor was raised?

13 What is meant by 'IRR of this project is 4.5%'?

14 State **three** qualitative factors that might influence a business investment decision.

Knowledge, understanding and application

Remember to use the appropriate method of investment appraisal and to calculate the net cash flows correctly for each year.

Sunshine Boat Builders (SBB)

SBB make luxury boats for the 'super rich'. Demand is currently very high for SBB boats. The directors are planning an expansion of the boatyard manufacturing capacity. Half of the cost would be financed by long-term loans. The new boatyard has to be near the river for the easy launch of new boats. There is no room to expand on the existing site so an additional location is being considered. The Managing Director prefers Site A – just three kilometres from the existing boatyard but in an area of great natural beauty. The Operations Manager prefers Site B – it is much cheaper as it is in a low-income country. The government of this country is keen to attract new industry. He comments, 'There is so much space for future expansion, the views of local residents will be ignored by the government and local workers are willing to learn new skills.'

The Finance Manager has estimated the net cash flows from these two alternative locations – see Table 36.1. The leases on the two sites will be for four years. When the Managing Director saw these figures, he was worried that the Finance Manager might not have considered transport and training costs. He asked the Finance Manager whether the forecasts had been adjusted for the extra risks involved in operating in another country.

Year ending	Site A	Site B
0	(20)	(12)
1	10	6
2	12	8
3	14	8
4	16	10

Table 36.1 Forecast net cash flows ($m)

15 Calculate the payback for Site A.

> **WORKED EXAMPLE**
>
> 1 year and 10/12 × 12 months
>
> = 1 year and 10 months

16 Calculate the payback for Site B.

17 Explain why a quicker payback might be of benefit to SBB.

18 Calculate the ARR for Site A and B. (Use: Average annual net cash flow/Capital cost × 100)

19 Comment on your results.

20 Using a rate of discount of 10%, calculate the net present value of these two sites.

Year	1	2	3	4
Discount factor at 10%	0.91	0.83	0.75	0.68

21 Calculate the discounted payback period on each of the two sites, using a 10% discount rate.

22 Compare these results to those from Q15 and Q16

Knowledge, understanding, application and analysis

Explaining the significance of investment appraisal results is an important form of analysis.

23 Analyse the payback and the ARR results.

24 Analyse why SBB might consider the NPV results to be more important for the final decision than either payback or ARR.

25 Analyse why knowledge of the IRR (internal rate of return) might be of benefit to SBB's managers.

> **WORKED EXAMPLE**
>
> IRR is the discounted rate of return on an investment. It is that rate of discount which when applied to the future net cash flows, will give a result of zero. The higher the IRR is, the more profitable the investment project is. **[K]** As Site B has a slightly quicker payback and a slightly higher ARR it might seem best to opt for this site. **[Ap]** However, it has a lower NPV – but this is not surprising given that it is a much cheaper project. IRR is not distorted by the cost of the project and it gives the true discounted rate of return, taking both the cost and future net cash flows into account. In this case it would allow a better way of comparing the profitability of these two projects. **[A]**

Knowledge, application, analysis and evaluation

The skill of evaluation requires that you make supported decisions, draw conclusions and give recommendations.

26 Assess which site the managers of SBB should choose based on both quantitative results and qualitative information.

27 Evaluate whether the information provided and the investment appraisal results calculated provide sufficient data for the managers to be confident about the choice of site.

> **TIP**
>
> For Q27, consider the likely accuracy of the forecasts, the relative importance of qualitative factors, and how IRR might help in the decision. Justify any additional information you think might be useful.

36 Investment appraisal (A Level only)

Exam-style questions

Paper 3

So Cool Cosmetics (SCC)

SCC specialises in soaps, hand and body products and perfumes made only from freshly picked, organic natural ingredients. Its main selling method is a TV shopping channel and several times demand has been so high that SCC sells out completely. This keeps customers waiting for the production operations to catch up with demand. The two partners who own SCC are considering an expansion of production capacity. Currently, most of the products are hand-mixed, using small-batch production, in large containers with basic mixing and bottling equipment. Labels are put on manually and the bottles and other containers are then packed by part-time employees ready for postage to customers.

The partners realise that this production method will have to change to meet demand. However, they disagree on the best alternative method. Sue wants to purchase Machine A, which would allow for flow production of the most popular products. It is fully automated and requires just one operator trained in IT. The machine labels and packages each container. This production process will need a continuous supply of raw materials.

Pat wants to buy Machine B, which would still use batch production but on a much larger scale compared with existing operations. It is semi-automated and will require more employees than Machine A to operate. Pat thinks that products could still be advertised as being 'mixed carefully by our skilled workers'. The machine will need thorough cleaning between batches of different products.

The partners have asked Pat's brother – a business consultant – to forecast the likely net cash flows from these two machines. They are both estimated to have a useful life of five years, after which they could be sold as scrap. His forecasts are shown in Table 36.2. He has warned the partners that interest rates might be increased by the Central Bank soon and asked them how they intended to finance the new machine.

End of year	Machine A	Machine B	8% discount factors
0	(150)	(85)	1
1	70	45	0.926
2	80	45	0.857
3	90	45	0.794
4	110	50	0.735
5	120	55	0.680

Table 36.2 Forecast net cash flows from the two machines ($000)

1. a Calculate the discounted payback period for both machines at an 8% rate of discount. **[2]**
   b Calculate the ARR for both machines. (Use: Annual average net cash flow/Capital cost × 100). **[4]**
   c Calculate the net present value for both machines at an 8% rate of discount. **[4]**
   d Comment on the investment appraisal results of the two machines. **[8]**

2. Recommend which machine SCC should buy. Justify your answer with reference to the investment appraisal results and other information provided. **[14]**

Improve this answer

This is a student's answer to Q2. Skills are shown in brackets to help you.

The discounted payback is slightly quicker for B and if the finance is to be borrowed then this makes it a better investment as slightly less interest will have to be paid on each dollar borrowed as it will be paid back faster. [K/A] However, the difference is very small. [Ap] The ARR for A is higher but we are not told what SCC's criterion rate of return is. It is likely to be less than the 42.67% ARR result – which seems very high so the forecasts might be inaccurate. More information about how these forecasts were obtained by Pat's brother would have been very useful. [Ap/E]

The NPV is much higher for A – but then we would expect this as it costs twice as much. The question is, what is the discounted rate of return – the IRR? This would have given a more realistic assessment of the future profitability of these two machines compared to the cost of buying them. [A/E]

Your challenge

This is an incomplete answer – and it could have been so much better. None of the points made are applied to the machines or the nature of the business or its products. There is no attempt to consider qualitative factors – such as the impact of automation on brand image and whether demand really is high enough to justify continuous flow production. The inadequacy of the data provided is hinted at – but more detail could have been given. Although some judgements are made – there is no overall recommendation. A better answer is available online – but write yours out first!

36 Investment appraisal (A Level only)

Unit 5 Research task

AirAsia Berhad

AirAsia is one of Malaysia's most successful 'low cost' airlines. Apart from operating many routes in Asia, it also has investments in an insurance business, Expedia the travel website, food processing and a leasing company. The leasing company specialises in helping airlines obtain new aircraft without the loss of liquidity associated with buying them outright. AirAsia is considering selling some of these assets to reduce borrowing and possibly increase dividends to shareholders.

In the three months to 31/3/16 AirAsia's gross profit margin improved significantly following a 29% reduction in jet fuel prices compared to the same period in 2015. At 1/1/16 the company had issued 2,782,974 million shares. It paid a dividend of 0.04 RM (Malaysian Ringgit) per share and its share price was 1.83 RM.

Simplified summary of financial information for AirAsia, 31/3/16 (RM 000)	
Revenue (3 months to 31/3/16)	1,699,294
Cost of sales [labour and fuel costs] (3 months to 31/3/16)	582,522
Expenses [including interest] (3 months to 31/3/16)	595,633
Operating profit (3 months to 31/3/16)	521,139
Non-current assets	16,408,213
Current assets	3,578,936
Inventories	38,324
Current liabilities	4,315,790
Non-current liabilities	10,670,758
Capital employed	15,671,359

Adapted from AirAsia published accounts [and The Star, Malaysia]

Write a report, aimed at ANY TWO stakeholder groups, about the performance and future prospects of AirAsia. You must:

1. use accounting ratios in your report

2. include in your report a comparison with either: i) the latest three-monthly period for AirAsia or ii) another airline – perhaps in your own country – for the three-monthly period ending 31/3/16 (or as close to it as data allows).

Unit 6
Strategic management

(A Level only)

Learning outcomes

The exercises in this chapter will help you to practise what you have learnt about:

- The meaning of strategic management
- Differentiating between tactical decisions and strategic decisions
- Analysing the importance of strategic management
- Discussing links between strategy and organisational structure
- Evaluating the importance of business strategy in gaining competitive advantage.

KEY TERMS

Corporate strategy	**Strategic management**
Tactic	**Competitive advantage**

Key skills exercises

Knowledge and understanding

To answer the questions in this chapter, you need to know and understand:

- **the meaning of strategic management and how it differs from the taking of tactical decisions**
- **links between strategic management and organisational structure (Chandler's views)**
- **the meaning of competitive advantage and how strategic management can add to it.**

1. Define 'strategic management'.
2. Give **one** example of a tactical decision and **one** example of a strategic decision made within a social media business.
3. Give **one** example of how a new strategy can influence an organisational structure.
4. Give **two** ways in which a business could gain a competitive advantage.
5. Give **one** example of a strategic decision that an airline could take to try to gain competitive advantage.

Knowledge, understanding and application

Remember to use the skill of application to help you put the analysis of the arguments you make into context. You also need to make sure that evaluative comments are directed towards the business in the case study.

Outdoor Clothing (OC)

Rajev is the Chief Executive Officer of OC, which is a public limited company based in country X. OC makes a very large range of specialist clothing for outdoor leisure activities. Examples of its range – all branded with the OC logo – include:

- shirts and dresses that are designed for use in very hot climates and which protect from the sun's harmful rays
- lightweight leisure clothing for people who enjoy walking and cycling
- ski clothing such as waterproof trousers, jackets and boots to protect skiers and keep them warm in very cold weather.

Rajev has just left a Board meeting with other directors – all heads of the main functional departments. They were discussing the three growth strategies which Rajev has recently proposed. After several years of falling profit, OC has managed to reverse this trend by cutting production costs by transferring most production to very low cost countries. OC is now one of the lowest-cost producers of specialist outdoor clothing in this increasingly globalised industry. However, OC's overall sales are not increasing, although some products are doing better than others. Country X's economy has been in recession but last month economic growth was recorded. The demand for most of OC's products is income-elastic. Rajev now thinks that the economic and market environment is right for growth strategies that will expand OC profitably. Rajev's three strategic options are:

Strategy A: Sell all OC products exclusively online and not through retailers. This would potentially give OC a higher profit margin but there would be costs involved too. Rajev is concerned about the impact on OC of a recent merger between two large retailers who currently sell a high proportion of OC's output.

Strategy B: Start selling the OC clothing ranges in country Y for the first time. Rajev has provided the directors with information to help in making this decision including the data shown in Appendix 1.

Strategy C: Purchase the patent and all manufacturing rights to an innovative new clothing material. The material is called 'Weartex' and is better than OC's famous synthetic material 'Litetec' that the company has used for many years in a range of products. 'Weartex' is claimed to be very lightweight yet completely waterproof and windproof. It can be washed easily and dries in minutes. It could open up opportunities for innovative and differentiated OC products.

Rajev wants the directors to make a choice soon about which of these three strategies should be adopted. He told the directors, 'We must take advantage of our low costs to achieve substantial sales growth to keep shareholders satisfied. We must move quickly because one of our major competitors has announced a technical breakthrough in the manufacture of synthetic materials which will cut its material costs by 50%. We cannot depend on being one of the lowest cost producers for ever. I have been in business long enough to recognise that one of these three strategies is right for OC. Detailed strategic analysis is unnecessary.'

Other important decisions

The directors of OC have some important decisions to take in the next few months. Apart from choosing between the three strategies, A, B and C, decisions have to be made about:

- Operations – should OC make substantial long-term changes to its manufacturing processes to incorporate lean production principles?
- Marketing – should prices of all clothing be reduced by 10% during the 'out-of-season' period?

37 What is strategic management? (A Level only)

- Finance – should fixed assets be depreciated by a greater proportion of their value each year?
- Human Resources – should many of the functions of this department be outsourced to a low-cost country, requiring the redundancy of over 125 employees, including middle and junior managers, and the sale of the large office building currently used by HR?

Country X	Country Y
Total population is rising by 4% per year.	Average incomes are rising by 8% per year, leading to more foreign holidays.
35% of the population is under 24 years old.	Building and construction industry is booming due to low interest rates.
A government-owned company has a monopoly in internet service provision.	Unemployment is falling.
Import quotas on imported electronic goods have been abolished.	Import tariffs have recently been increased by government.
Business property taxes on city centre shops have recently increased.	Currency is appreciating against most other currencies.

Appendix 1 Selected economic and social data for country X and country Y

6. Differentiate between tactical decisions and strategic decisions by using examples from the case (other than Strategy A, Strategy B and Strategy C).
7. What type of strategy has OC been adopting to gain competitive advantage?
8. Outline any **two** factors that might influence the future corporate strategy of OC.

> **WORKED EXAMPLE**
>
> Finance is one of the sources that will influence OC's future strategies. **[K]** Strategy C might be expensive and OC's profits have been falling – so internal finance might not be available. **[Ap]**

Knowledge, understanding, application and analysis

The skill of analysis requires that you explain reasons for a possible outcome or consequence of a decision.

9. Analyse how Strategy B might affect OC's organisational structure.

Cambridge AS and A Level Business

> **WORKED EXAMPLE**
>
> OC is organised along functional departments and seems to have a hierarchical structure. **[K]** We know this because outsourcing HR responsibilities will involve the loss of many middle and junior managers' jobs. **[Ap]** Strategy B will require a structure that manages the operations in country Y. One option is to have a team of managers from each functional department with responsibility for managing operations in country Y. This geographical structure could be semi-independent to increase delegation and to ensure that the marketing and cultural differences in country Y are reflected in OC's operations in that country. **[A]**

> **TIP**
> For Q12, analyse the nature of strategy and strategic management, why it is important to this business's future and why the uncertain business environment might mean that any strategic decision does not guarantee future success.

10 Analyse how **two** of OC's functional departments might be affected by Strategy A.

11 Analyse **two** ways, other than those outlined, in which OC might further improve its competitive advantage.

Knowledge, application, analysis and evaluation

The skill of evaluation requires that you make supported decisions, draw conclusions and give recommendations.

12 Discuss the importance of strategic management to OC's future success.

Exam-style questions

Paper 3

1 Discuss how business strategies could determine OC's competitive advantage in an increasingly competitive world. **[20]**

Improve this answer

This is a student's answer to Q1. Skills are shown in brackets to help you.

The world's markets are becoming increasingly competitive due to globalisation, which is mainly encouraged by free trade agreements. A business must take important business decisions to survive. Very often these decisions are strategic in nature – such as selling in other countries, diversifying or increasing product differentiation. [K] According to Porter the two main ways in which a business can gain or retain competitive advantage is through either low costs or effective product differentiation. [K]

Low costs would allow a business to keep prices very low and become competitive that way. [A] Differentiation means making your product so different and so desirable that price becomes much less important. [A] Low costs of production are not necessary with this second strategy. Differentiation is used by Swiss watch makers, for example. These businesses can price products at many thousands of dollars and still be profitable and successful. [A] However, it can be expensive to differentiate products and services as research and development might have to be undertaken and the product supported by a massive promotion campaign. [E – but not awarded marks as it is not applied to OC]

37 What is strategic management? (A Level only)

Your challenge

See whether you can improve on this answer – which does have some important strengths, as it clearly shows understanding of competitiveness and how this might be achieved. One very important part of a successful 'discuss' answer is missing, however. There is no application to the case study, which means that the answer lacks evaluation. A better answer is given online – but write yours out first!

38 Strategic analysis (A Level only)

Learning outcomes

The exercises in this chapter will help you to practise what you have learnt about:

- Understanding what strategic analysis means
- Analysing a business using SWOT and PEST and assess the limitations of these techniques
- Evaluating the role of business vision and mission statements in strategic analysis
- Analysing product portfolios using the Boston Matrix
- The significance of Porter's 5 Forces and core competencies analysis as a framework for business strategy.

KEY TERMS

Strategic analysis	Vision statement
SWOT analysis	Boston Matrix
PEST analysis	Core competence
Mission statement	Core product

Key skills exercises

Knowledge and understanding

To answer the questions in this chapter, you need to know and understand:

- the meaning of strategic analysis and the main techniques used
- the main features of SWOT and PEST analysis
- the difference between vision and mission statements
- Porter's Five Forces analysis, Boston Matrix and core competencies.

1 Explain why strategic analysis should be undertaken before strategic choice.

2 State **one** purpose of a vision statement.

3 State **one** purpose of a mission statement.

4 Which aspects of SWOT analyse the internal features of a business?

5 Give **one** example of **four** factors that would be considered during a SWOT analysis for a social networking business.

6 What is meant by the 'Boston Matrix'.

7 State the **four** factors that, in Porter's model, contribute to competitive rivalry.

8 What is meant by the term 'core competence'?

38 Strategic analysis (A Level only)

Knowledge, understanding and application

Remember to use the skill of application to help you put the analysis of the arguments you make into context. You also need to make sure that evaluative comments are directed towards the business in the case study.

Refer to Case Study in Chapter 37.

9   Outline **one** strength of OC.

10 Outline **one** weakness of the OC.

11 Outline how political/legal factors might affect OC.

12 Outline how **two** economic factors might affect OC.

> **WORKED EXAMPLE**
>
> One economic factor could be exchange rates. **[K]** As Strategy B involves selling OC products to country Y for the first time, a depreciation of country Y's exchange rate would make OC products more expensive there than originally planned. **[Ap]**

13 How could 'Weartex' become a core competence for OC?

14 Suggest a mission statement for OC.

15 If one product in OC's ski clothing range has a low market share in a fast growing market, within which section of the Boston Matrix can it be classified?

Knowledge, understanding, application and analysis

The skill of analysis requires that you analyse reasons for a possible outcome or consequence or explain how or why something is a benefit or a limitation.

16 Analyse **two** benefits to OC of having the mission statement suggested in Q14.

17 Analyse **two** limitations to a SWOT analysis undertaken by the Chief Executive of OC.

18 Analyse **two** social factors which could affect OC in future.

19 Analyse how OC's competitive rivalry might be affected by:

   a a merger between two large retailers which currently sell OC's products

   b a technological advance that makes the manufacture of synthetic clothing materials much cheaper.

> **WORKED EXAMPLE**
>
> **b** This increases the threat of substitute products being developed and it might also reduce barriers to entry. **[K]** If buyers of outdoor clothing now prefer the clothing ranges produced using this cheaper material, then competitive rivalry increases for OC. **[Ap]** If new businesses are encouraged to come into this market because it is now cheaper to produce and use synthetic materials in outdoor clothes then, again, competitive rivalry increases for OC. As this market becomes more competitive, OC might consider other strategies to improve its competitive position. **[A]**

Cambridge AS and A Level Business

20 Using the data in Table 38.1 and Boston Matrix analysis, analyse **two** decisions that OC could take to improve the performance of its product portfolio.

OC product	Market share in country X	Annual market growth in country X
'Snow Coat' ski jackets	5% (6% last year)	15%
'Snowshoo' boots	15% (8% last year)	20%
Leisure walking trousers	2%	3%
'Sun stop' shirts	25%	4%

Table 38.1 Marketing data for four OC products

> **TIP**
> For Q21, explain the purpose of strategic analysis and how two or three techniques of strategic analysis could be useful for OC in this case. Evaluate the effectiveness of these techniques.

Knowledge, application, analysis and evaluation

The skill of evaluation requires that you make supported decisions, draw conclusions and give recommendations.

21 Assess the importance of OC undertaking strategic analysis before considering which strategic growth options should be considered.

22 Evaluate the significance of the Five Forces forces model and Prahalad and Hamel's core competence analysis to OC as a basis for future business strategy.

Exam-style questions

Paper 3

Hybrid Power Solutions (HPS)

HPS is a public limited company specialising in the manufacture of hybrid power systems for buses and trucks based in a European country, X. Hybrid power systems use both petrol-driven engines and electric motors to drive a vehicle. They are much more environmentally friendly than just petrol engines alone. Political, legal and environmental changes in many markets are requiring bus and truck operators to use hybrid engines. The long-term corporate mission of HPS is to 'develop unrivalled hybrid engine technology and create power solutions for the next century'. The core competence that HPS has gained in hybrid engines is also put to effective use in the company's power systems for boats and trains.

Summary of SWOT analysis for HPS completed by business consultant

Strengths	Opportunities
Well-known brand Patented hybrid engine designs Committed workforce	New markets for existing power systems, e.g. small ones for cars Transfer production to low-cost country Increase share in existing markets
Weaknesses	**Threats**
Long time to develop new engine systems Ageing workforce High production costs	Competitive rivalry from US manufacturers Price wars could drive down profit margins

Summary of PEST analysis for HPS completed by business consultant

Political:
- Pressure to make even hybrid engines illegal in city centres
- Change of government expected next year with plans to increase social security spending

Economic:
- Interest rates might rise
- Country X's currency expected to depreciate

Social:
- Pressure group activity against large vehicles on roads
- Demand for personal car transport still increasing

Technological:
- Some engine makers working on hydrogen power systems that would make hybrid engines out of date
- Danger of HPS patents and designs being copied and produced more cheaply

Strategic options

The directors are considering two strategies for future growth:

Strategy 1: Take over a small manufacturer of buses in a 'BRICS' country. This manufacturer does not currently use HPS power systems. It has designed a new large bus that is cheap to build and expected to be popular in lower-income countries.

Strategy 2: Establish a joint venture with R and P, a USA-based hybrid engine manufacturer, to design and manufacture a new generation of environmentally friendly engines to compete with 'hydrogen' ones. The venture would be based in an operating base in an African country and, if successful, could lead to rationalisation of existing production capacity.

Quantitative and qualitative data regarding these two options are shown in Table 38.2. Both strategic options would require careful implementation to achieve success as they both carry risk and would involve long-term commitment of substantial HPS resources.

	Strategy 1: Take-over bus manufacturer	Strategy 2: Joint venture with R and P
Estimated cost	$200m	$150m
Forecast IRR (over five years)	15%	20%
Greatest risk factor	Lack of synergy	Research fails to develop innovative product
Estimated chance of strategy failure	30%	20%
Expected (net) monetary value if successful (over five years)	$90m	$100m
Greatest constraining factor	Lack of HPS directors' experience in bus manufacture	Culture clash with USA business managers
Greatest driving factor	Increase sales of HPS engines to this BRICS bus manufacturer	Developing low-cost operations in an African country
Ansoff's classification	Diversification (although in related industry)	Product development

Table 38.2 Data comparing the two strategic growth options

Cambridge AS and A Level Business

Annual world GDP per capita growth	5%
European Union labour costs – annual growth	8%
BRICS labour costs – annual growth	2%
Average increase in global interest rates over period	4%
Growth in global market share of BRICS bus manufacturers	12%
External costs: EU maximum permitted pollution level per bus/truck engine in 2024 (2016 = 100)	65

Table 38.3 Global economic forecasts, 2018–24

1. Assess whether the SWOT and PEST data provided is sufficient strategic analysis to allow HPS to consider appropriate options for future growth. **[20]**

2. Evaluate two techniques of strategic analysis, other than SWOT and PEST, that HPS would find useful when considering appropriate options for future growth. **[20]**

Improve this answer

This is a student's answer to Q1. Skills are shown in brackets to help you.

SWOT analyses the internal and external factors that will influence the future direction and success of a business. [K] It helps to suggest or formulate appropriate strategies for the future. SWOT is useful in this case for identifying key internal strengths of HPS such as the committed workforce. This can be really important especially to the maker of a technological product where motivated employees and a low labour turnover can increase labour productivity. [Ap/A] On the other hand, the ageing workforce is a problem as to replace skilled workers who retire could prove difficult. This might make a joint venture operation in an African country, with a large and youthful population, a good strategy to adopt. [Ap/A]

The external opportunities also indicate potential future strategies especially developing hybrid power systems for cars. This could use the 'core competence' of HPS in another sector of the vehicle market and would appear to be a viable option for the future. [Ap] The external threats are serious and HPS may need to protect itself from these by, for example, insisting that patents are observed and intellectual capital retained in the business. This might need to be done before considering any future strategies for growth to allow existing operations to remain profitable. [A]

PEST analysis looks beyond HPS and analyses market and 'macro-environment' conditions. [K] It seems that pressure group activity and possible legal changes will continue to increase the demand for the most environmentally friendly engines – but complete vehicle bans would be bad for HPS. [Ap]

The economic conditions have a rather conflicting effect on HPS. Higher interest rates will increase the cost of loans for a new strategic option. However, as the business is a public limited company it might be able to raise capital from sale of shares and reduce the company's dependence on loans. [Ap] A currency depreciation will make country X's exports cheaper abroad so the export of hybrid power systems to a BRICS country will make that bus operation more profitable. [A]

So it is clear that the SWOT and PEST analysis provide really useful data that allows HPS directors to consider a range of strategic options for the future. Strategic analysis such as this is essential before the choice of appropriate strategies is made. [E – but not awarded marks as needs to be applied]

38 Strategic analysis (A Level only)

Your challenge

Although this is quite brief for a Section B essay, there are some good insights here. The answer avoids trying to refer to all of the data and is selective. This is an important strength as it allows the student to say 'more about a few things' than not much about many things! The answer is well applied and shows good analysis. It lacks detailed evaluation and this could have been shown by assessing the limitations of SWOT/PEST, considering what other techniques of strategic analysis are available and why the data they provide could be even more useful to HPS managers. See whether you can improve on this answer. A better answer is given online – but write yours out first!

39 Strategic choice (A Level only)

Learning outcomes

The exercises in this chapter will help you to practise what you have learnt about:

- The importance of strategic choice to strategic management
- Using Ansoff's Matrix model to analyse strategic choices and evaluate the model
- Analysing strategic choices using force-field analysis and evaluating the model
- Applying the decision-tree technique to strategic choices and evaluating its usefulness.

KEY TERMS

Ansoff's matrix
Market penetration
Product development
Market development
Diversification

Force-field analysis
Decision tree
Expected value

Key skills exercises

Knowledge and understanding

To answer the questions in this chapter, you need to know and understand:

- the meaning of strategic choice and the main techniques used
- the structure of Ansoff's matrix and the way in which it classifies strategic choices
- the main components of Force Field analysis and how this is used
- the concept of decision trees, how these are constructed and their main features.

1. Why do businesses have to choose between strategic options?
2. Differentiate between market penetration and market development.
3. Which of the **four** growth strategies is the riskiest?
4. Give a recent example of product development.
5. Differentiate between 'driving forces' and 'restraining forces' in force-field analysis.
6. State **one** limitation of force-field analysis.
7. Why are probabilities an important part of a decision tree?
8. Define 'expected value'.
9. State **one** limitation of decision trees.

39 Strategic choice (A Level only)

Knowledge, understanding and application

Remember to use the skill of application to help you put the analysis of the arguments you make into context.

Refer to the OC case study in Chapter 37.

Additional case study material

The OC Project Manager has undertaken an analysis of the three strategic growth options. He has estimated much of this data but he has also consulted with other HPS directors. See Figure 39.1 and Table 39.1.

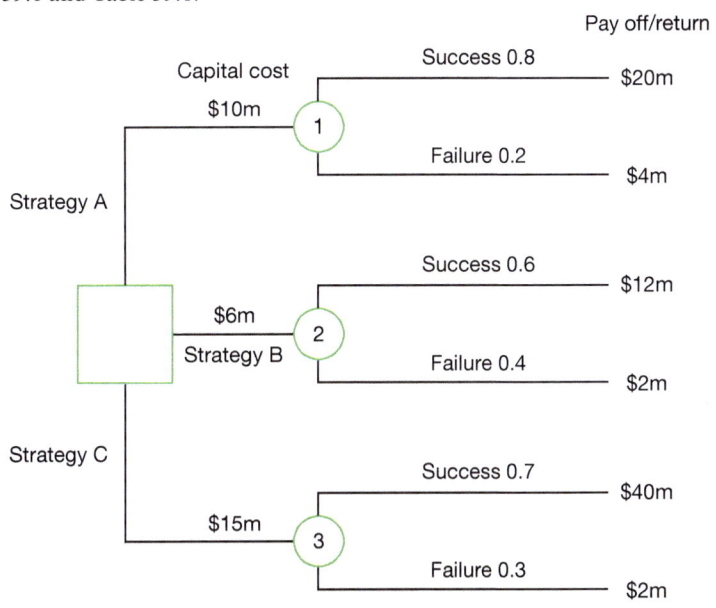

Figure 39.1 Decision tree for three growth strategies (financial returns for first five years)

Decision tree:
- Strategy A: Capital cost $10m → Node 1: Success 0.8 → $20m; Failure 0.2 → $4m
- Strategy B: $6m → Node 2: Success 0.6 → $12m; Failure 0.4 → $2m
- Strategy C: $15m → Node 3: Success 0.7 → $40m; Failure 0.3 → $2m

Pay off/return values shown on right.

	Strategy A	**Strategy B**	**Strategy C**
Summary	Sell all OC products exclusively online and not through retailers	Start selling the SC clothing ranges in country Y for the first time	Purchase the patent and all manufacturing rights to 'Weartex'
Ansoff's classification	See answer to Q10	See answer to Q10	See answer to Q12
Major constraining forces and values (out of 10)	Sales representative job losses (6) Website set-up costs (8)	Language barriers (5) Cultural differences (7)	Employee training to produce material (6) Cost of patent (8)
Major driving forces and values (out of 10)	Social trend of online buying (8) Lower advertising costs (5)	Country X market maturing (4) Booming economy (5)	Competitive pressures (5) Customer demand for new materials (9)
Force-field overall scores C = constraining forces D = driving forces	C = 32 D = 35	C = 33 D = 29	C = 30 D = 33

Table 39.1 Analysis of the three growth options

10 Classify Strategy A and Strategy B according to Ansoff's matrix.

11 Outline an example of a strategy that would be a form of diversification for OC.

12 If Strategy C is adopted and leads to the development of several non-clothing products, how would it be classified in Ansoff's matrix?

13 Comment on the different outcome probabilities for the three strategies.

14 Calculate the expected value at the nodes 1, 2, 3.

> **WORKED EXAMPLE**
>
> Node 1 = ($20m × 0.8) + ($4m × 0.2) = $16.8m

15 Outline how any **one** driving force for each strategy could be increased.

16 Outline how any **one** of these constraining forces could be reduced.

Knowledge, understanding, application and analysis

The skill of analysis requires that you explain how or why something is a benefit or a limitation.

17 Analyse **two** benefits to OC of using Ansoff's matrix.

18 Analyse **two** limitations of the decision tree that OC's Project Manager is using.

19 Analyse **two** uses of the force-field analysis OC's Project Manager is using.

20 Analyse **two** limitations of the force-field analysis.

> **WORKED EXAMPLE**
>
> One limitation is that the allocation of values to each constraining or driving force can be subjective. **[K]** Why did 'language barriers' obtain the value it was given? **[Ap]** If these values prove to be inaccurate then the benefits of using force-field analysis are much reduced and other techniques become more important. **[A]**

Knowledge, application, analysis and evaluation

The skill of evaluation requires that you make supported decisions, draw conclusions and give recommendations. You also need to make sure that evaluative comments are directed towards the business in the case study.

21 Recommend to OC's directors which of the three strategic growth options the business should adopt. Justify your recommendation. Refer to Table 39.1 and other information in your answer.

> **TIP**
>
> You need to select data carefully – do not try to comment on all data available. Analyse some data for all three strategies. Evaluate the data and the techniques used. Make an overall decision – explain why you have made this decision and why you reject the other strategies.

39 Strategic choice (A Level only)

Exam-style questions

Paper 3

See HPS case study Chapter 38

1 Recommend to HPS's directors which of the two strategic growth options the business should choose. Justify your recommendation. Refer to Tables 38.2 and 38.3 and other information in your answer. **[20]**

Annotate this answer

This is a student's answer to Q1.

Strategic choice is a very important part of strategic management. Taking poor strategic decisions can result in business failure. Much is at risk with HPS as failure to respond effectively to increasing environmental concerns and the threat of 'hydrogen' engines could lead to years of low growth and low profit. The capital cost is $50m higher for Strategy 1 and this could cause financing problems for HPS. If cash is not available internally then a share issue or a loan will be required. A share issue could dilute control of existing owners and a loan will increase the gearing ratio, adding to the risk of the investment. It would have been helpful to have investment appraisal results other than IRR as if the payback is quicker for Strategy 1 than 2, then the additional initial investment might not be that significant for this plc.

Risk is a key element in this case as neither option is market penetration – the least risky growth strategy. A high risk reduces expected values on the decision tree and this could be why the expected value is less for Strategy 1 than 2. Although buying a bus manufacturer keeps HPS in a related industry to hybrid power systems, building buses in a low-cost country, thousands of kilometres away from the base country, is a completely different operational situation to building complex power systems in Europe. The fact that 'lack of synergy' is the biggest constraining factor in force-field analysis suggests that there is a real risk that these two manufacturing businesses, when integrated, will not offer the cost or marketing benefits that might be expected.

There are risks and uncertainties with Strategy 2 as well. US and European management cultures are not the same and there is a real danger that there could be a clash of management styles that prevents this new joint venture from working. For example, each group of managers might assume that they are the ones in overall charge of this new engine project. Setting up operations in an African country might offer a keen and youthful potential workforce but it will need training to be effective and there might not be any local suppliers of components. This might add to the overall cost of the project. In addition, product development is always potentially risky. It might not be physically possible to devise a new type of engine which is even more efficient and environmentally friendly than the new hydrogen-powered one being developed by competitors. In such a case, the investment will be largely wasted. Innovative products do not always result from research and development.

Overall, I would recommend OC to choose Strategy 2. It is cheaper, has a higher discounted rate of return (IRR) and offers a higher monetary value, after deducting the initial cost. The data in Table 38.3 contains some of the most convincing evidence. Although the demand for BRICS built buses is forecast to grow, environmental pressures (especially in the EU) mean that these new buses will need even more efficient and 'greener' engines than the current hybrid ones. These engines could come from Strategy 2. Also, the rapid growth in EU labour rates suggests that an African manufacturing base for a newly developed power system will offer significant cost savings.

However, before making a final decision I would expect more detailed information such as the estimated payback period of both projects and much more information about how the risks and financial data were estimated. These techniques are only as accurate as the data they are based on. I am not confident that these forecasts from the Operations Director are totally reliable – especially as he seems in favour of Strategy 2 to start with.

Your challenge

You should, hopefully, identify this as being a good answer with effective application to HPS and detailed evaluation. The final conclusion is well supported – but there are some qualifying statements about the data provided too. The answer avoids trying to refer to all of the data and is selective. An annotated version is online – but mark your copy with the skills of K, Ap, A and E first!

40 Strategic implementation (A Level only)

Learning outcomes

The exercises in this chapter will help you to practise what you have learnt about:

- Understanding why strategic implementation is an important part of strategic management
- The importance of business plans and corporate planning to strategic implementation
- Corporate cultures and the impact they can have on strategic implementation
- How a change culture can be established and how businesses can manage and control change
- The importance of contingency planning and crisis management.

KEY TERMS

Strategic implementation
Business plan
Corporate plan
Corporate culture
Power culture
Role culture
Task culture
Person culture

Entrepreneurial culture
Change management
Business process re-engineering
Project champion
Project groups
Contingency plan
Crisis management

Key skills exercises

Knowledge and understanding

To answer the questions in this chapter, you need to know and understand:
- **the meaning of strategic implementation**
- **the benefits of planning – business plans and corporate plans**
- **different types of business culture**
- **the benefits and limitations of contingency planning.**

1. Explain why the process of strategic management is not complete until strategic implementation has occurred.
2. List **four** major sections of a business plan.
3. List **two** benefits to a business from corporate planning.
4. State **two** possible limitations of corporate planning.
5. What is meant by 'corporate culture'?
6. Differentiate between 'task culture' and 'person culture'.
7. What is meant by 'entrepreneurial culture'?
8. Differentiate between managing change and leading change.

9   State **two** important changes that have occurred in recent years within an industry of your choice.

10 List **four** stages in contingency planning.

Knowledge, understanding and application

Remember to use the skill of application to help you put the analysis of the arguments you make into context.

Additional OC case study material (see also Chapters 37 and 39)

OC's Operations Management department operates three factories in low-cost countries. Factory workers have very little job security and can be dismissed for minor mistakes. They are only expected to do the job they have been shown how to do and they must not argue with the Production Supervisors – who take their orders directly from Production Managers. In contrast, the clothing design department employs 15 independently minded clothes designers. They are encouraged to think up creative and innovative designs of outdoor clothing. Each designer is praised if their designs are successful but if they are not they are still encouraged to take risks with other new designs.

Rajev has instructed the HR department to operate a 'hard' HR strategy to cut costs. The Finance department is being encouraged to window dress the accounts to impress shareholders. Rajev has even spoken to the Marketing Director about suggesting that 'sale' prices offer even bigger discounts from the original price than they actually do.

FIRE IN OC FACTORY

Last week a serious fire destroyed part of an OC factory. Three workers were killed and thick black smoke from the fuel stores caused breathing problems in the local town. Production has still not restarted. Some retailers are short of supplies of OC clothing. All production and HR records for the factory were lost in the blaze. Workers are now complaining that they do not know what will happen to them. Suppliers have just been told to stop sending trucks full of materials with no explanation why. At a press conference Rajev was reported to say that: 'We were taken completely by surprise so it's no wonder that things are still in a bit of a mess. We will put everything right soon so there is no need to worry.' When a major investor in OC heard these comments, he immediately informed the Board of OC that unless Rajev was quickly replaced as CEO, his investment company would sell all of its OC shares.

Today, the Board announced that it: 'regretted Rajev's sudden departure and that the search for a new CEO would start immediately'.

11 Outline **two** benefits to OC of business planning when implementing any **one** of the possible growth strategies.

12 Identify the corporate culture in the Operations Management and Clothing Design departments.

13 Outline **two** ways in which the CEO could lead the changes necessary if Strategy A is chosen.

14 Outline **two** reasons why the crisis caused by the fire was handled so badly.

40 Strategic implementation (A Level only)

> **WORKED EXAMPLE**
>
> One reason why the crisis was badly handled is that there appeared to be no contingency planning. **[K]** 'We were taken by surprise' suggests that OC's managers never even considered the possibility of a factory fire and therefore did not plan for this contingency. **[Ap]** Contingency planning would have given managers experience in what to do and they would have reacted much more quickly than they did. **[A]**

Knowledge, understanding, application and analysis

The skill of analysis requires that you explain the benefits and limitations of different business techniques and models and the consequences of business decisions.

15 Analyse **one** benefit to OC of having a clear vision if it chose Strategy C and had to implement it.

16 Analyse **two** reasons why leading change and not just managing it are important to OC if Strategy B is chosen.

17 Analyse **two** problems OC are likely to experience from not planning for contingencies.

18 Analyse **two** possible benefits OC might experience from changing its corporate culture.

> **WORKED EXAMPLE**
>
> Benefit 1: Under Rajev's leadership OC's culture seems more interested in cutting costs and increasing returns to shareholders than looking after other stakeholders. **[K/Ap]** Factory workers are paid low wages, some marketing employees might lose their jobs with Strategy A and customers might be misled by the 'sale' pricing claims. **[Ap]** A corporate culture that put people first and not profit might lead to good publicity, a positive brand image and a quicker response to crises. **[A]**

Knowledge, application, analysis and evaluation

The skill of evaluation requires that you make supported decisions, draw conclusions and give recommendations. You also need to make sure that evaluative comments are directed towards the business in the case study.

19 Evaluate how the new CEO could implement the necessary changes within the business assuming that Strategy A is chosen.

> **TIP**
>
> For Q19, explain the business changes needed within OC if Strategy A is chosen, for example large increase in IT employees, and direct contact with customers so OC must have, for example, social media systems in place to deal with these contacts. Rajev's culture would probably have led to poor leadership – will the new CEO have the qualities needed to change culture too?

20 Discuss whether changing the culture of OC should be the first priority for the new CEO.

Cambridge AS and A Level Business

Exam-style questions

Paper 3

Additional HPS case study material (see also Chapter 38)

Last week, news reached HPS head office that one of its latest hybrid engines, fitted to a truck, had exploded in a busy town centre. No one was injured but the driver of the truck was lucky to escape the fire that resulted from the explosion. HPS directors immediately called a press conference to explain what action they intended to take. Customers who had trucks fitted with the same model of engine – 230 trucks in total – were asked to take them off the road. Compensation was offered for loss of business. Production of this type of engine was halted and factory workers told that they would be paid in full even though they had no work to do. The exploded engine was shipped back to HPS's engineering division and within 24 hours of this the cause of the problem had been analysed. A faulty hose connection had allowed petrol to pour onto the electric motor. The supplier of the hose was told to produce an improved hose as soon as possible – this took just three days. The owners of the 230 trucks were informed that the new hose would be fitted free of charge. HPS took out large advertisements in transport newspapers to reassure future customers about the quality of their products and that this was the first serious incident involving an HPS hybrid engine since they were introduced 12 years ago.

Media reports did not criticise HPS engines – they praised the speed with which the company had responded to this crisis. The CEO was reported as saying: 'The way we respond to crises like this is more important for the future of HPS than any new power supply invention.'

1 Evaluate how HPS's directors could implement successfully either of the two strategic options. **[20]**

2 Evaluate the statement from the CEO that 'the way we respond to crises like this is more important for the future of HPS than any new power supply invention'. **[20]**

Annotate this answer

This is a student's answer to Q1. Skills are shown in brackets to help you.

Strategic implementation means putting a strategy into effect in a planned way with the purpose of reaching a desired objective. Both of these options are major strategic decisions involving significant change and substantial resources. Detailed corporate and departmental planning will be needed including contingency planning. For example, a political crisis in the country where the buses are manufactured could prevent production from continuing. HPS will need to plan for this and other eventualities and the distance between the country and where HPS is based will make handling 'disasters' more difficult.

Adequate resources must be prepared, especially finance and people. Both options will require much finance and HPS must plan for this or it might face liquidity problems later. A share issue, as it is a plc, could possibly be sufficient to provide the finance needed for either option. Employees with foreign language skills might be required for either option (e.g. the language spoken in the BRICS or African country might not be the same as the language spoken within HPS). HR recruitment strategies must take this into account. HR could undertake a workforce audit to see if any existing employees have foreign language skills or have expressed an interest in working overseas.

These options may take away vital resources from HPS's existing operations which could be damaging especially as the business is getting over the hybrid engine explosion.

40 Strategic implementation (A Level only)

Managing these resources will be important. However, of even greater importance will be the need to lead the change. A clear vision will be needed to reassure workers, shareholders and other stakeholders that HPS has a clear objective and sense of purpose for whichever option is chosen. The directors will have to explain the reasons for the chosen strategy and the objectives of it – to employees and other stakeholders. For example, Strategy 2 seems to fit in best with the original mission statement of HPS so the vision for this strategy would be well understood by most stakeholders.

Successful implementation of either strategy will be vital to success of HPS as failure could put at risk the entire business given that it faces increasing competitive rivalry from the company developing the hydrogen engine.

Your challenge

This is another good, if rather brief, answer. Annotate it – using K, Ap, A and E. You can check the annotation online but mark your copy first!

Now that you have completed all of the questions in this book, you should be able to differentiate between these four important skills.

Unit 6 Research task

Airbus and the importance of strategy

For Airbus, as one of the world's leading manufacturers of commercial aircraft, staying one or more steps ahead of the competition is critical. There is no magic 'crystal ball' that can predict aviation trends short- or long-term. Airbus therefore relies on an empowered Strategy team that influences all aspects of the company and its global operations.

At the centre of this Strategy team is Dr Kiran Rao, Airbus's Executive Vice President, Strategy and Marketing. Setting out Airbus's overall approach to preparing its future, Dr Rao first explained why a single person is in charge of the two activities.

'To put it simply, these two departments are inextricably linked,' he said. 'Marketing is about understanding how our products meet the needs of customers and Strategy is about anticipating how those needs will evolve and proposing products and services adapted to their future business environment and the world they operate in.' Dr Rao continued: 'A major product change can take five years, a completely new aircraft eight or more. And then they'll be flying for 30 years, so we have to think ahead.'

The Strategy team's specialists identify trends by analysing the company's strengths, weaknesses, opportunities and threats. Then current market trends and competitors' actions, macro-economic forecasts and future infrastructure developments (such as new airports) are assessed.

Recently, the strategic decision has been taken to sell off some subsidiaries of the business so that Airbus can use its core competences to focus on its core products – mainly commercial aircraft.

'Some business areas are identified as divestment candidates as they do not fit the strategic goals,' the company said. These include communications businesses such as commercial satellite activities.

Adapted from Airbus.com and IndustryWeek.com

Write a report to the Directors of Airbus or another major multinational company, containing:

a   a brief SWOT analysis of the business

b   an analysis of at least **two** recent strategic decisions taken by the business

c   an assessment of how future strategies could be used to maintain the competitiveness of the business.